The Agape Bloom

The Sacred Ceasefire Of The Mind

Leeanne Meikle

Book 1 of Series

Copyright Page

ISBN: **978-1-0671194-0-9**
First Edition 2025

Dedication

To my brothers Stephen Meikle ("Stevie")   1971 - 2019

Darrin Meikle ("Baby Blue") 1974 - 1997

To my adult children - Shannon, Daniel, Kelsey, and Tre - who understood too early in life that loving can hurt, trust can be broken, and deep loss is a reality. This is *our* journey.

You are my seeds, planted innocently in depleted soil, with Agape as our guide - finding our way home to full Bloom.

"The privilege of loving you is stronger than the human pain of tremendous loss."

"To every soul who has long suffered quietly and still hopes for peace - this book was written for you. May this work remind you that your bloom is always possible".

— Leeanne Meikle

Foreword

Every so often, a book arrives that does not add more noise to the conversation of healing, but instead clears the space so that truth can be heard again. The Agape Bloom is such a book.

In a world overflowing with methods, techniques, and ever-expanding self-help frameworks, the message here is startling in its simplicity: peace is not something we must earn, achieve, or build. It is already here - quiet, steady, waiting beneath head noise & distraction.

What *The Agape Bloom* offers is not another practice to master, nor another ritual to maintain. It offers a reminder: that our perception of life is created by thought, and thought is temporary. When we stop treating every thought as truth, we rediscover what cannot be broken - the truth of *who* we are.

This return is one of reconnection. Not only of the mind, but of the whole self - body, mind, and (heart centre) spirit. It is how we rest, how we nourish our bodies and souls with kindness instead of criticism. These habits are difficult to maintain when we are stuck in survival (burned out from prolonged overstress and nervous system dysregulation). We often beat ourselves up for not being disciplined enough, for being inconsistent when we try and seemingly 'fail' over and over again with practices and rituals that are helpful and offer excellent support to our wellness.

The Agape Bloom is the gentle reconnection to spiritual truth. It provides the simple *how-to*, without the overload of more information often pitched by self help, healing practices, and rituals. It is not a theory to practice. It becomes a lived *experience* that changes everything!

For this reason, I have reserved the optional guides including some rituals and practices within the Appendices that may be helpful for some to experience the *'sacred ceasefire of the mind'*.

The core message of The Agape Bloom is found within its chapters. This transformative 'message' is based on simplicity and ease. It is the missing piece of the puzzle for sufferers of overwhelm, self-help seekers & the spiritually or therapy fatigued who *know intuitively* that there has to be an easier way to emotional freedom.

Authors Note

Long before our time, the ancient Greeks gave names to love. They spoke of **Eros** ~ romantic love, passionate and fiery. They named **Philia** ~ the love of deep friendship, of shared trust. They described **Storge** ~ the steady love of family, the bonds of belonging.

And then, there was **Agape**.

Agape was not tethered to condition or circumstance. It was not earned by effort or withdrawn by failure. It did not demand, measure, or cling. Agape was seen as the highest form of love ~ unconditional, expansive, free. Love that simply *is*.

It is this word, its living truth, that fertilizes the root of **The Agape Bloom.**

The sunflower is The Agape Bloom's living metaphor. Planted in any soil - even heavy with toxins - it grows toward light. Its beauty does not come from effort or striving but from alignment with what is true.

So it is with us.

This book is not about fixing what is broken, you will come to understand what can never truly be broken. It is about reconnecting with what has remained, buried beneath the stories we accept as truth. Agape is both the root and the bloom: when you live in alignment with unconditional love and truth.

An Invitation

Agape is not earned. It does not wait until you are perfect, healed, or unscarred. It is here, now. Unconditional love is not a natural human state - even within the closest of human relationships - parent and child. All humans operate from their perceived reality. Ego vs Truth. Those who are mindful and connected to this greater understanding, *know* the difference.

This is what many call living from a state of higher consciousness.

The Agape Bloom is your invitation to discover this for yourself. To reconnect all parts of yourself in *love* without condition. To live in *truth* without fear. To rest in the gift of *peace* without striving. And to allow *joy* - that quiet gladness of being alive, to rise naturally.

May you discover that what you are seeking has never left you.

Table Of Contents

Appendices

Welcome, New Friend.

We may not have met in person, but if you have come across this book, I believe we were meant to connect.

This is not a textbook, or a manual. I am not an academic. I hold no degrees, no formal training, no shiny title to present as authority. What I carry is my lived experience: a long history of loss, overwhelm, disconnection, burnout, and the heavy belief that I was "too much, or not enough." I suffered under the weight of false guilt, shame, and misdiagnoses. For many of those years, I was drowning - barely keeping my head above water.

So yet, here I am: alive, present, free. Living proof that lasting transformation is possible despite years of suffering endless loop patterns typical of mental un-wellness. I was labeled with interwoven diagnoses at different times throughout my life. To discover, with hindsight - they were not fully accurate, though innocently adopted as truth, at the time.

The knowledge I share within these pages comes from lived experience and insights passed down by wise teachers. These words are for anyone inflamed by life, overwhelmed by chaotic thinking, drowning in cycles of depression, anxiety, or loss; for those who feel disconnected from themselves and from life itself ~ and most importantly - those who are *ready* to come home to peace.

The Agape Bloom is my contribution to your journey, and the fulfillment of a promise I made to my youngest brother, Darrin, the year he died by suicide in 1997. Twenty-eight years later, that promise now lives in your hands.

My brother Stevie, who also took his life in 2019, once said: "If people judge mental illness, that doesn't make them stronger or superior. It just makes them lucky."

I agreed with him. Some people in life simply strike it lucky. For many of us, despair can arrive like a thick, unrelenting cloud. In those times, thoughts feel like iron bars - cold, rigid, permanent. The mind whispers accusations so cruel at times, and we believe them. Thought echoes inside our heads. They feel absolute.

I devoted decades to personal growth and healing. I did "the hard work." I gained tools to manage my inevitable cycles of unraveling - but I *knew* something was missing. The endless patterns of repeated struggle - striving, crashing, gasping for air - became an expected torment I knew I needed to brace for.

The profound shift in my healing journey was when I discovered Fiona Lukeis and her *Relatable Program*, online. The principles she shared revealed a truth that had been there all along: I was never broken. I was never meant to live enslaved to my own thoughts. This new understanding was the missing piece of the puzzle I had long sought. I often tell her that the understanding she teaches with simplicity and clarity is a 'gift that keeps on giving'. The Agape Bloom is part of that gift.

This understanding broke the life-long chains that repeatedly threatened my existence. It was not dramatic, but deeply personal ~ gentle, undemanding, utterly transformative. It was the moment of coming home to myself. What I had perpetually believed about myself was never the truth ~ only a story I had rehearsed for decades..

And stories can change.

When I came across Fiona Lukeis's work, I was exhausted. Tired of excuses, tired of automated patterns sabotaging my life. I had tried countless modalities. Each brought relief, new skills on how to manage thought and emotional spirals. However, despite being *able* to name the 'root problems' I had no solution on how to be free from them.

I longed for permanent change. A reset. I simply wanted *freedom. Consistency.* For a brain that would support me, not cause my unravelling. What set me free was surprisingly effortless - there was no reliving of trauma via discussion, no digging up or even mentioning the past, no endless analysis.

It was a fresh, simple insight - a clarity that bypassed the clutter of my mind and landed in something deeper. I discovered that lasting transformation requires the following:

Not more knowledge, but *deep knowing.* Something *remembered in the heart,* not just understood intellectually. What I will share with you requires an openness to possibility. It goes against much of what we believe or have been taught.

A Missed Opportunity

Ironically, I had encountered a similar teaching in my late twenties. At the time, I was diving into psychology based therapy groups, counselling, and self-help books. I found psychology expansive and eye opening. I was a sponge! While attending a work related development course, I considered the mindset-based teaching ignorant, lacking in compassion and understanding - so I rejected it outright. *I knew better.* They didn't understand my journey. They lacked information.

Looking back, I see the truth: we cannot welcome new understanding while clinging tightly to our stories, justifications or old beliefs. Time has taught me that belief is not fixed - it bends, expands, when we are ready, then we make space for new understanding.

I spent twenty-five additional years trapped in debilitating spirals before I finally heard wisdom clearly again - and this time, I was ready.

I don't want that long road for you. My hope is that you *open* - even gently - to the possibility of freedom now.

A Different Way

This book does not ask you to peel back endless layers, revisit trauma, or fight your "shadow." While those paths may serve some, this is a different way: fresh, simple, gentle, powerful, sustainable. It is the path of least resistance.

The Agape Bloom is not about fixing what you believe is broken. It is about *reconnecting* to an *immovable truth*: you were never broken at the core of your essence. You may feel broken. I know I did. Beneath the noise, you will find that your natural state has always been whole.

Like the sunflower planted in heavy toxic soil, you were designed to rise, to turn toward light, to bloom.

A Gentle Invitation

This is your journey. There are no rigid steps, no rules.

You will notice, The Agape Bloom presents a non-linear reading experience. There are no formal chapters, just titles and page numbers. I invite you to wander through the symbolic field of pages. Intuitively, with an open heart and mind. Trust that you will be drawn to what you need, when you need it. If something resonates, stay with it. If it does not, let it go. Move forward.

You are not alone. We walk together in this - discovering that the weary sufferer can heal, the over-giver can find balance, and the burned-out soul can come home to peace.

So let us begin. With curiosity. With honesty. With simplicity.

You are precious.

You deserve *the sacred ceasefire of the mind* this understanding can bring.

New possibilities, peace, and love in abundance await you.

Agape,

Leeanne Meikle

The Bloom Remembers

Once, I thought I would break.

The weight was too much,

the soil too heavy,

the darkness unending.

But I see now

I was never buried to die.

I was planted to rise.

The cracking open of the seed within

It was not the end.

It was

the beginning of a new life.

The Sunflower ~ The Muse

The sunflower is more than a flower of beauty. It is a healer, a survivor, and a teacher.

After devastation - when soil is poisoned with toxins, especially in disastrous nuclear spills - this golden bloom is planted first. Its roots reach deep, drawing heavy metals from the earth, cleansing what was spoiled. It will contain the toxins until it is cut down, and handled as radioactive material. It fulfills its purpose and is then discarded. Its natural state is tall, golden, turned toward the sun - steady, luminous, and free.

Planted In Depleted Soil

The plant cannot choose its soil. It absorbs whatever surrounds it - nourishment or toxin, gentleness or harshness. Survival leaves its mark.

So it is with the one who suffers emotionally. A child raised in chaos, silence, or unpredictability grows with a nervous system already on guard. Stress chemistry surges where safety should have lived. Their body learns to scan, to brace, to bend - long before it learns to rest.

And yet, like a seed buried in darkness, potential waits. Blueprinted within every seed is the instinct to rise. Even in poisoned ground, the shoot moves toward light. *As do we.*

The Science

Research shows that children raised in unpredictable environments often develop hypervigilance - the body tuning to danger even in harmless moments. The heart races. Muscles stay on guard. Cortisol and adrenaline surge. The child absorbs the atmosphere of the home as if survival depends on it - because it does..

In its early life, the young bloom bends constantly, tracking the sun from east to west as if afraid to lose the light. With maturity, that urgency fades. It finds its still point - rooted, trusting, steady - waiting each dawn to greet what it no longer fears will leave.

From bending to belonging. From absorbing poison to releasing what doesn't belong. From chasing connections to discovering our own integration. This is our mirrored journey.

For this reason - this bright, tall and resilient flower is the muse of *The Agape Bloom*. It reminds us that even planted in poisoned ground, a full life and purpose can return. Suffering is not weakness; it can become wisdom. The light we chase is already within us, waiting for us to stand still and remember.

The Sufferers Body & Mind

When we live under prolonged emotional, mental, or physical stress, the body begins to communicate in a different language. The calm rhythm governed by the parasympathetic nervous system - rest, digestion, repair - is replaced by the storm of fight, flight, or freeze.

When stress is unresolved, the body's emergency system forgets how to turn off. Stress can be *distress* or *eustress*. Commonly understood, *distress* is harmful and negative in nature, and *eustress* is helpful i.e. energetic, purposeful, motivating. You feel capable, present, engaged. It is linked to excitement. *Here's the thing;* The body does not label stress as good or bad. From the brain and nervous systems point of view -

eustress and distress use the same chemical pathways of adrenaline, nor adrenaline, and cortisol.

Eustress becomes equally damaging when a person never down-regulates, when one's body is kept in chronic sympathetic activation (always on high), urgency and achievement become a constant. Where stillness is avoided because it feels uncomfortable or unproductive. The body says '*Stay on alert*'. Over time the body adapts by raising the baseline.

This sounds like " I feel most alive when I'm busy" or "Slowing down feels unsafe or empty" and "Rest feels like a loss of identity". So the adrenaline fueled individual prefers to stay energised, driven, needed, productive, and inspired. Until the body says "NO!"

The statistical results - burnout, anxiety, auto-immune issues, emotional numbness, physical, mental or emotional collapse. These results are the body's brakes.

Hormones once meant to protect us begin to erode us - fueling inflammation, exhaustion, and disease.

Healing is not only emotional; it is physiological. It is the integration of mind, body, and spirit returning to its natural balance.

When the mind perceives threat or helplessness, the HPA axis releases cortisol and adrenaline. In short bursts these protect us. When stress is prolonged and chronic, the system no longer resets. The body remains on high alert - chemistry overwhelming immunity, digestion, mood, cognitive and cellular repair.

This is what Bessel van der Kolk meant when he wrote that trauma "gets stored in the body." It's not metaphor - it's measurable biology.

The Chemistry of Disconnection

The body and brain are in constant conversation - a dance between gut, heart, and mind. Science calls this the gut-brain axis, a living communication network carried through the vagus nerve, neurotransmitters, and hormones.

When calm returns, this axis flows. The gut produces approximately 90% of our serotonin. Dopamine moves through balanced pathways, restoring motivation and joy. Oxytocin reminds us we belong.

Under prolonged stress, this delicate system falters. The gut becomes compromised; the microbiome loses diversity. These organisms help produce the very chemicals that regulate emotion. Without them, our inner weather shifts: flatness, anxiety, lack of motivation - this is clearly a contributing factor to mental un-wellness. The body is not failing. It is adapting for survival.

It simply hasn't been told the inner war is over.

Healing Through Reconnection

Healing accelerates when the body starts to feel safe again. Every act of calm signals, *"you can rest now"*. Slowing down in all we do, when we eat, do our chores - being intentionally slow, including our breathing, has proven to lower cortisol.

Every gentle pause, from a mindful stroll amidst lush garden or bush, to slowly savouring the flavour from our fork, slowly tells the vagus nerve that danger has passed. Over time, this rhythm rewires the brain, restoring the natural dance of thought, emotion, and physiology.

"Peace is not created by effort. Peace is revealed when thought slows, and you allow every part of yourself to follow suit"

* See Appendices & Bibliography for further information

Heliotropism – Chasing the Light

In youth, the sunflowers bloom bends anxiously from east to west, chasing the sun. This remarkable adaptation helps it grow strong, but it is also restless. The young plant does not yet trust the rhythm of its source. It fears the light will leave, so it naturally pursues it.

Post traumatic sufferers often do the same. Innocently, they do not yet trust their inner guidance. Instead, they bend toward others - scanning for cues of safety, approval, or love. Conditioned by early uncertainty, the nervous system learns to chase connection wherever it appears. Tilting, twisting, adjusting - hoping to secure belonging and safety. Outward validation becomes fuel.

But bending has a cost. The body and mind become weary. The spirit depletes. Eventually, one must learn what this resilient bloom knows when *fully* mature: the light is constant, and it cannot be lost. We have simply forgotten our way.

The Science

Part of attachment theory shows that children raised in unpredictable environments often develop anxious attachment. As adults, they may over-give, over-please, or over-adapt, fearing abandonment if they do not. The same dysregulation can occur later in life when an individual is exposed to prolonged unpredictable environments, whether in the home, workplace, and even toxic cultural and religious settings. Despite a safe upbringing. Much has been written about prolonged toxic environments and the post trauma response.

Neuroscientific studies confirm this pattern: the brain wires around the fear of disconnection, scanning faces, tones, and silences for danger. Even neutrality can feel like rejection. This is why so many come to believe they must earn love. I personally know this too well. I am aware of these automated patterns within myself, and gently acknowledge the role I innocently perform within all of my meaningful relationships when I forget '*who I am*'.

Awareness and acknowledgement is enough, to gently guide us back to our center and choose differently. This is the grace within Agape - we do not need to perform or be 'perfect', to remain unconditionally loved and supported. *Agape* is our anchor. Be kind to yourself when you see your old patterns emerge. See them as a gift. It's simply part of our human conditioning. (*not* who we are) Wisdom will guide us to greater freedom every time we see clearly, and choose differently.

What Earning Love Looks Like:

- Adjusting ourselves moment by moment to keep others comfortable
- Softening opinions, changing energy, or over-explaining to prevent perceived disapproval
- Becoming 'emotionally fluent' in others while losing connection to ourselves

- Anticipating needs in others before being asked
- Becoming indispensable
- Proving worth through usefulness
- Being easy, agreeable, low maintenance
- Becoming whoever we sense the other person wants

What Over-giving & Self Sacrifice Looks Like:

- Giving more time, energy, emotional labour or resources than is sustainable.
- Saying "yes" automatically, even when exhausted
- Feeling guilty for needing rest, space, or reciprocity

What People-Pleasing & Self Abandonment Looks Like:

- Avoiding conflict at all costs
- Withholding own needs, preferences, or truth
- Taking on blame quickly, even when unsure

- Agreeing outwardly while feeling resentful or unseen inside

We can choose to relate authentically, and from a place of kindness to ourselves once we see in "that" instance our shift from center to over-extending, or shrinking. This is the power of clarity, truth and love. We are guided every step of the way, when we stay connected to our inner wisdom through intuition.

A Seed Of Agape

You have bent yourself long enough. You do not need to chase to keep love.

The light will always return and it was never outside you.

Rooted Stillness

As the plant matures, something changes. It no longer bends anxiously. It settles into steadiness. At full growth, it turns eastward and waits - rooted, ready each dawn to greet the light.

This is wisdom. A *quiet knowing* that the source will return.
 No striving. No chasing. Simple trust.

We, too, can arrive here. After years of bending, scanning, absorbing, we can discover that peace is not earned through effort. Peace comes through stillness, through self aligned trust, through letting the nervous system root itself again in safety. The question is how?

The Science

The body lives in two primary modes: survival and rest. Chronic stress locks a person into survival - cortisol surging, muscles tight, mind exhausted. But as the nervous system relearns safety, the parasympathetic system activates.

The heart slows. Digestion restores. Inflammation cools. Thoughts soften. The body remembers safety.

A Seed Of Agape

There is a still point beneath your storms. You were never meant to bend forever.

Peace is not 'out there'. It is here, within, waiting for you to come home.

The Turning Point

This is the turning point - a shift from survival to renewal. From carrying what harms, to standing in natural design: tall, rooted, steady.

Humans meet this same threshold. Years of absorbing pain - our own and others' - that have overwhelmed the body, mind, and spirit. To continue is to burn out. To lose hope. Survival alone becomes unbearable.

This is the sacred question:
Do I keep carrying what was never mine, or do I release it and return to safety?

The Science

Psychology names this the breaking point - when old strategies collapse and the cost of self-sacrifice becomes too high. Without change, the risks are chronic illness, shutdown, emotional or mental collapse. Biology agrees: the body cannot live in constant overdrive. Excess cortisol damages organs, exhausts the brain, and dulls joy. Release is not indulgence - it is physiology.

A Personal Note

Many of you know this breaking point - not once, but perhaps repeatedly. I have personally experienced this on several occasions.

My first mental breakdown came at age twenty-five. It was also my first brush with suicidal ideation. For six months, I could not function normally. I was a Christian wife and mother of three young children, with little support. Well-intentioned people told me to *pray more*, to have stronger faith.

Depression, they said, was a poor witness for Jesus. The pressure to perform, to people-please, to be "enough" crushed me further. Seeking professional help outside of the church was strongly discouraged.

My breaking point was not failure. This was the weight of a system I was never meant to carry. It was the beginning of wisdom rising - the first crack of light.

A Seed Of Agape

Inevitably, there comes a time when carrying must cease
A moment when the soil of others - and your own inherited
scripts - become too toxic for your roots. Again, this is not
a failure. This is wisdom. It is the call to begin your bloom.

Part II

The Inner Landscape

From Noise to Freedom

When despair takes hold, thoughts feel heavy, permanent, and absolute. They shout so loudly that it becomes easy to forget what they truly are - thoughts, nothing more.

Consider this: every feeling we experience begins with thought. And both are temporary. Thought moves, shifts, and dissolves. It is not a permanent reality. For those living with a constant deregulated nervous system, a racing mind, or an emotionally heightened state - it *feels* permanent. Feelings are real. However, as you may come to realise, they are rarely accurate as guidance when we are deregulated.

The noise in the mind grows crueler, louder, and more chaotic in times of stress and tiredness. Somehow, we innocently believe thought. We follow its commands. We wear its accusations like a cloak and *mistake* them for truth.

For those living with ADHD, Bipolar, BPD, depression, or anxiety, this mental turmoil is magnified. The inner chatter doesn't just nag; it aggressively abuses and belittles the sufferer. In our darkest states - emotions don't just sting; they consume. It can feel as if the entire experience is being played out on a stage for the world to witness. And the longer we entertain these stories, the more real they appear - and the more often they return.

Repetition carves grooves in the brain. Neurologically, we walk the tracks of whatever we think most often. And so the story continues. It becomes 'our story'. Our *identity*. Our lived *reality*.

What I am about to share is not new. This wisdom has been shared for thousands of years. It is not loud nor complex. It is simple.

Once seen, it cannot be unseen.

Once grasped, suffering no longer holds the same power - because *you* do.
And the life you reclaim is not the one you lost, but something better. So much better!

This understanding runs counter to much of popular psychology, which teaches that a big part of recovery requires endless processing of trauma - feeling deeply by revisiting pain, analysing every layer, dissecting every wound. Thankfully, many leading voices, including Dr Gabor Maté and Dr Joe Dispenza, are shifting this narrative with approaches that relieve, rather than deepen the burden on the sufferer.

I know without a doubt that what we focus on grows. I have lived this truth. Many former sufferers have discovered it too, and with this knowledge, they have become more aware of where their attention and energy is directed.

It is easy to become dependent on modalities that promise healing. They may bring temporary relief, but soon the old patterns return. We chase the next practice, the next breakthrough, while the quiet seed of hope within us waits - unseen, and forgotten. That seed has always been there. It only needs to be acknowledged, gently tended to release the potential you already *sense* within.

After decades of struggle, I am deeply grateful to see differently now. The years I spent exhausting myself just to stay afloat were misguided - innocent, but misguided. Every glimpse of "getting better" was swallowed again by familiar internal scripts and behaviours that fed my cycles of despair.

That cycle - gasping for air, then being dragged back under by old undercurrents - is where suffering further cemented. Most people who have battled long-term mental un-wellness understand this cruel cycle.

These episodes are not always triggered by life's circumstances, but by the power unknowingly handed to memory-based thinking - the mental noise we innocently assume is truth.

I witnessed this in my beautiful brother Stevie, who suffered over many years, as did I. The cycles were exhausting, relentless. The sufferer screams internally for release - for quiet - for peace. Too many we have loved have lost this battle. And silent, they became.

Are you ready to discover the simple yet profound truth that transformed this *former* ADHD, CPTSD, overthinking, chaotic, exhausted sufferer? *(yes, former)* The chapters ahead share the understanding that gifted me with lasting emotional and mental freedom. Yes, triggers and patterned thinking still visit. The difference is - I *know* my way home, back to my present moment, my natural state of peace.

This wisdom continues to grow and expand daily. It is not difficult. There is no discipline, pressure, or rigorous practice. Only a simple shift in focus and an openness to see differently.

My Turning Point

The understanding I share in the pages ahead grew from a simple yet profound recognition - a moment where my entire being said *Yes*. An insight. An epiphany. The 'Aha moment', as Oprah famously penned. The moment I experienced with precision "I am *not* my thoughts' (Eckhart Tolle). This insight changed *everything*. I had, for years - innocently identified with 'who I *thought* I was' shaped by the accusatory, repetitive thought narratives. I was living from *inside my head* - I'm certain you can relate. This was my then, permanent home. My reality.

Today, with tears of gratitude, I can say: I am free. I have my life back - no, something far greater than I ever imagined. Anyone who has lived under the merciless weight of overthinking, negative looped internal narrative, or mental un-wellness knows the magnitude of these words. To be free from debilitating spirals after decades of imprisonment is beyond language. The word *gratitude* barely touches it.

I am whole. Not because I tried harder. But because I choose to be intuitively led (heart centred). I now get the power of choice *if* and *how long* I suffer for. I rarely make myself available to the dramatic emotional 'climate' of external and internal scripts that no longer belong in my life. My old patterns did not serve me; they conflicted me.

The loudest voice - *my thinking* - was never the truth. Doctors, therapists, even those who loved me added their perspectives, but the deepest prison was always this: *believing all my thoughts and feelings were accurate.*

Begin To Notice

Freedom begins when you start to pay attention.
Not to fix. Not to fight nor negotiate. Simply begin to notice your thinking. Ask yourself gently: *What is the tone of this thought? Where is it coming from?*

When you step back, even for a moment, you begin to see the thought for what it is - random, irrelevant, and often distorted, stitched together from memory or fear. It is not *'truth'*, as you will come to realise. It is usually old news, almost like gossip - especially when the body and nervous system are tired or triggered by stress or memory.

Once you form the habit of noticing thought, and seeing it clearly - you may even smile at your choice not to give it so much of your attention. Instead of agreeing with thought in that moment - speak to it kindly by saying *'I see you'*. Choose presence over distraction. And thought is often that - a distraction.

The Shift

The moment you stop feeding "mind chatter," with attention, it begins to slow. The intensity and speed in which it repeats reduces. Not unlike the calm after meditation or yoga - yet all you have done is notice the chatter and declined to give it your attention.

As this recognition continues, as you practice *'noticing'* you find that space opens within your body and mind for something new.

When we do this, we create space for fresh information, *a quieter voice*, a certain *knowing* from within can enter. This is your inner wisdom - insight/intuition. Soon you will understand: *this* inner wisdom - *you can trust*. This is where truth resides. We will discuss the layers of truth in a later chapter.

This inner wisdom is never pushy. *Never* unkind. It does not demand. It guides - gently, steadily. Everyone has access to it, though many do not know how to recognise it.

This is what many call our higher consciousness. This quiet space expands us into greater awareness we never realised we had.
This is the beginning of reconnection to your true essence. A remembrance of who you *really* are.

You will know it when you know it.

Over time, this becomes more familiar; as attention to thought lessens, the mind settles. *This is the sacred ceasefire of the mind.* Where the mind *surrenders* to the wisdom of the heart. You may begin to notice what has always been there: the stillness beneath everything, the way light falls through a window, the warmth of laughter in your chest, and the beauty of *simply* being here. Also known as *presence.* Gratitude arises naturally. Joy rises without effort. Peace that defies logic becomes your new norm. This is what Eckhart Tolle - and countless other teachers before him - have taught - *being in the now.* This is true freedom. This is coming home.

A Seed Of Agape

The despairing mind believes its thoughts are truth. Wisdom whispers differently: negative, accusatory thought is not based in truth - half-truths at best - it usually dredges up the past or creates fear of the future. When we realize we can choose the lens we see through, at any moment, suffering softens. And in that clarity, the heart-centered self discovers the immovable truth "I was never broken. I was only believing my thoughts - borrowed, distorted, and never the truth of who I truly am."

A Simple Practice

Thought Watch: Today, notice three thoughts th

Feelings – The Echo of Thought

Feelings are not random currents washing over us. They are the faithful echo of our thoughts in the moment. Like ripples formed in a lake when you throw a pebble, they appear in direct response to what our mind projects.

This is why feelings can seem so convincing. The body responds as if every thought were true. A fearful thought quickens the pulse. A joyful thought lightens the moment. The chemistry is real, but the source is always upstream - our *thought*.

Sydney Banks often said: *"Thought is the missing link between the spiritual and the physical."*

When thought moves through us, it creates form (energy) in our awareness. *Feeling* is that form taking shape in the body. It is the proof of thought's presence, *but rarely* of external reality.

Why This Matters

When we mistake feelings as signposts of truth, we fall into confusion. We may believe, *"I feel anxious, therefore something must be wrong."* But the feeling is not always proof of danger. It is more commonly, the echo of the thought we are entertaining at the exact moment.

Seen in this light, feelings are not enemies or obstacles. They are gentle guides. They point back to thought, reminding us: " You are *'thinking'* this way right now." *Nothing more.* No need to follow its direction. *Just notice.*

The Gift of Seeing Through

The moment we recognize the link between thought and feeling, a quiet freedom dawns. We no longer need to fight our emotions or fix them. Instead, we let thought settle, as it naturally does when not fueled by our attention. When the mind clears, feelings shift of their own accord.

Experiment with this.

When we are conditioned by complicated therapy and modalities, digging up past trauma to reveal the root issues in our lives, this *(not so)* new understanding almost appears too simple or dismissive. Remain open, and simply notice.

Peace is not something we manufacture. It is what remains when we embrace this understanding and allow the storm of thought to pass, as it always does when we don't take it so seriously.

A Simple Practice

Next time a strong feeling grips you, pause and ask:

What thought is giving rise to this feeling?

Is that thought necessarily true?

If I let this thought pass like a cloud in the sky, within my mind, what happens to the feeling?

You may notice a softening. Perhaps not instantly, but with patience, the echo of feeling quietens as the thought is seen, not entertained or fueled with a stress response.

A Seed Of Agape

Feelings are a real human experience and lifelong companions, but not always reliable guides to truth. I understand this is contradictory to what we have been told. Stay with me here.

Intuition is different. We can rely fully on intuition when we learn how to decipher the difference.

Feelings simply mirror thought in real time. When this is understood, drama loses its grip. What once seemed overwhelming becomes a passing rain cloud. It's a natural occurrence. Nothing more. Nothing less.

The Two Guides ~ Feeling and Intuition

Imagine you are standing at a crossroads. Two guides appear beside you.

The first is Feeling. She speaks quickly, almost breathlessly.

Her stories are vivid, dramatic, and urgent. She insists, "This path is dangerous! No, that one is better! Wait - maybe you should turn back!" Every word she speaks causes confusion. Sometimes she makes you hopeful, sometimes fearful, but often restless.

The second is Intuition. She does not rush to speak. She waits until the noise of the first guide begins to fade. Then, in a voice that is calm and steady, she simply points and says, "This way."

She offers no explanation, no drama, no panic. Yet something in you recognizes the truth of her direction. It feels lighter, clearer, as if you already knew.

In situations of imminent danger, she is strong, focused and direct.

The Nature of Each Guide

Feeling is fueled by thought. Every story she tells is born from the mind's chatter. She is not trying to deceive you - she is just echoing what thought is saying in that moment. But because she speaks with such energy, she can be mistaken for truth.

Intuition is not born of thought at all. Her guidance comes from the deeper intelligence of life, the place beneath the noise. She doesn't argue or persuade. She **_knows._**

Walking with Awareness

If you follow *Feeling,* as your guide - you may zigzag from one path to another, never quite arriving. If you wait for the guide - *Intuition,* the way forward feels simple, almost obvious.

Both guides will appear in your journey, but only one leads to peace and inner truth.

Five-Minute Practice: Telling the Guides Apart

Step 1 – Pause the Noise

Find a quiet spot. Close your eyes. Notice the swirl of thoughts and the feelings they stir. Acknowledge them: "That's Feeling, telling her stories."

Step 2 – Listen Without Acting

Let the feelings rise and fall without trying to fix them. See how they shift, just like clouds moving across an expansive blue sky.

Step 3 – Ask the Question

Gently ask yourself: "Beneath all of this, what do I quietly know?" Don't force an answer.

Step 4 – Notice the Difference

If what arises feels urgent, dramatic, or anxious - that's still *Feeling*.

If what arises feels calm, simple, and clear - that is *Intuition*.

Step 5 – Trust the Whisper

Breathe in deeply. Exhale slowly. Allow the quieter knowing to stand on its own. It will never shout, but it will always feel lighter.

A Seed Of Agape

Thought & Feeling is the weather - dramatic, changing, and loud at times. Intuition is the sky - steady, clear, and always there. When you know the difference, you can let the gossipy guide talk herself out and wait for the quiet one to point the way home.

Inner Dialogue

Authors' Hindsight

There was a time when my world was ruled by thought and feeling, that felt absolute, cruel, and unrelenting. They sounded like the truth, but they were not. They were echoes of pain, exhaustion, and a nervous system caught in survival.

A Daily Invitation to Come Home

The invitation is simple.

Do not judge your thoughts. Do not argue with them. And certainly do **not** believe the ones that reduce, criticize or condemn you.

Simply *notice* them. Smile at them. See them as echoes - not reality.

What we fuel with our focused attention grows. Positive or negative - thought shapes our experience. When the body is dysregulated and the mind speeds up - looping over and over, thought cannot be trusted as a guide.

Do this instead.

Everytime you notice 'thought' - remember to just let it gently be - instead of giving it full attention. As you do this from a place of observing rather than participating, you step closer toward the quiet place within - where wisdom awaits.

Slowly and over time - everything shifts. Notice what happens when you begin to do this. Be gentle with yourself. You are creating new habits. Learn to approach this with playfulness.

The following examples are the pattern of thoughts that once kept me enslaved and disempowered. Paired with the deeper truths that quietly waited beneath them, and also the hindsight I can now offer those suffering.

1. "I can't go on anymore."

Truth: *This feeling comes from thought. Thoughts pass, but life remains. Life is still here, waiting for you.*

Author's Hindsight: I remember this heaviness well. My mind replayed old stories, my body and brain were burned out from trauma and years of poor self-care. My nervous system was shattered. I believed this thought many times. Today, I know the truth. I am living proof that things can get better when we reconnect to our inner truth - truth that is deeply rooted in unconditional love.

2. "Nothing will ever get better."

Truth: *That is the illusion of a tired mind. The seed of possibility is within you - nurture it.*

Author's Hindsight: Everything shifted when I realised freedom was closer than I believed. I don't have to engage every thought or feeling that drags me down. The choice is now mine.

3. "I am broken beyond repair."

Truth: *You feel broken - but that is only a story of thought.*

Author's Hindsight: My nervous system was dysregulated, my body exhausted, and my mind caught in endless loops. However, I was never truly broken - simply exhausted from suffering. Thought and feeling were convincing, but not accurate.

4. "I'm a burden to everyone."

Truth: *That is belief, not truth. Your presence carries the same sacred value as every soul.*

Author's Hindsight: That voice was fear and learned self-hatred. Now I know my presence adds light, just as anyone else's. My lens was distorted then. I couldn't see myself through truth or unconditional love.

5. "No one could ever understand me."

Truth: *Thought isolates, but love unites. You are not as alone as you feel.*

Author's Hindsight: Heart-centered awareness showed me that suffering is universal. Most are disconnected and wrestle with thought - and everyone can be free when they see through it.

6. "I don't matter."

Truth: *That is despair speaking. Your life holds sacred value simply because you exist.*

Author's Hindsight: I remember believing this often. Today, I know my value doesn't need proof. Existence itself gives me worth.

7. "I can't escape my pain."

Truth: *Pain lives in thought, and thought shifts moment by moment. What feels unbearable now will soften.*

Author's Hindsight: My suffering came from believing my thinking. It struck mercilessly at times. But when I began to listen to inner truth - not the critic in my head - I noticed peace was already present beneath it.

8. "I'm too tired to keep fighting."

Truth: *You don't need to fight. When you stop struggling with thought, peace rises naturally.*

Author's Hindsight: Exhaustion was my constant companion. The real battle was within my mind. When I stopped resisting and stopped giving cruel thoughts my attention, I watched them loosen their grip. They now pass - like illusory clouds. They have no substance. Just temporary.

9. "The world would be better without me."

Truth: *That is a cruel illusion of thought. The world is touched by your being in ways unseen.*

Author's Hindsight: I truly believed this once. I thought leaving this world would spare my children pain. That's how distorted the sufferer's mind can become. What I once saw as weakness and shame has become my gift. The world is richer with me here.

10. "I'll never heal."

Truth: *Healing happens in the now, not in the mind's timeline. You are alive - healing is already in motion.*

Author's Hindsight: I suffered cruelty from others at times in my life. Trauma is real. But the suffering that haunted me - lived in memory, thought, and fear - all past, yet felt real in the present. PTSD does this. Now I choose awareness, presence, and truth. Thought and feeling can be cruel dictators to trauma survivors, but I no longer fuel or obey them. Peace and self-kindness are my allies. I accept all parts of myself. I choose what I focus on and release the rest. This is my power. I live peacefully.

11. "My past has ruined me."

Truth: *The past is memory, not reality. You are free here, now.*

Author's Hindsight: My past no longer defines me. Painful thoughts have no hold on me. Even suffering taught me compassion. I hold the key to my freedom.

12. "I'm trapped with no way out."

Truth: *There is always a way - a new thought, a new perspective, a new moment.*

Author's Hindsight: The trap was never outside me - it was in my thinking. Once I saw that, freedom came quickly. I've been free for years now, after decades of cyclical suffering. I once thought this impossible.

13. "I'm worthless."

Truth: *Worth is not earned. Worth is your essence, untouched by thought or circumstance.*

Author's Hindsight: My worth is unshakable. Nothing can add to it or take it away. I am as sacred as the trees and the breath of life in motion.

14. "I've lost myself."

Truth: *The self you long for was never lost. It waits beneath thought.*

Author's Hindsight: I was always here - buried under layers of pain and rehearsed stories. The trauma was real, its effects undeniable - but so was my release. I am free now.

15. "I'm too damaged to love or be loved."

Truth: *Damage is only a story of thought. Love is your nature.*

Author's Hindsight: I once feared I wasn't enough. Now I know I am both loving and loved. No thought can take that truth from me.

16. "I can't trust anyone."

Truth: *Distrust is born of fear. When thought quietens, the heart remembers connection.*

Author's Hindsight: Trust began when I trusted myself. From there, trust in others followed. If that is broken, it doesn't change my worth - it only reveals their humanness.

17. "There's no point to living."

Truth: *That is thought clouding vision. Meaning is revealed in being alive, here and now.*

Author's Hindsight: The point of life is life itself - the small joys, the quiet acceptance of sorrow, the beauty of ordinary moments. We can't control life's storms, but we can choose how we meet them. And it's okay not to be okay. "There is no point in living" is thought at its cruelest.

18. "My feelings are unbearable."

Truth: *Feelings are tied to thought - and all feelings pass, no matter how strong.*

Author's Hindsight: Even my darkest feelings shifted. Feelings are powerful storytellers, but not always trustworthy guides. When they disconnect me from love or peace, I know not to believe them.

19. "I've wasted my life."

Truth: *That is judgment from thought. Life is never wasted - every breath is sacred.*

Author's Hindsight: Nothing was wasted. Even my suffering taught depth and compassion. Today, I'm grateful to share hope with others, to know connection and wholeness.

20. "I don't see a future."

Truth: *The future is imagination, not reality. All you ever have is now - and peace lives here.*

Author's Hindsight: This moment is enough. Fear of the future once consumed me, but now I smile at my humanness. Thought passes when I stop fuelling it. Peace is my chosen state. Gratitude is my life expression.

A Seed Of Agape

In despair, the mind insists its thoughts are truth. But wisdom knows thought is never reality - only fear dressed as certainty. When thought quiets, clarity rises. And in that clarity, the whole self remembers:
There is so much more available to me than I realised. I innocently believed my thoughts.

Part III

The Living Truth

A Living Thread Through Time

Ancient Beginnings

From the time humans could be recorded, many have looked for strength not in what happens to them but in how they meet it.

Again and again, through every age, voices rise with the same reminder: freedom begins in the heart-aligned mind, in the way we choose to see. You may resonate with these 'insights' shared from famous historic figures.

Marcus Aurelius quotes emphasize control over one's mind, focusing on inner peace, and living virtuously.

His quotes include: *"You have power over your mind - not outside events. Realise this and you will find strength."*

Also - *"The happiness of your life depends upon the quality of your thoughts"* and *"The best revenge is to be unlike he who performed the injury"*

These and the following quotes echo still, reminding us: peace was never outside, but always within.

The Shaping of Perspective

As centuries turned, others carried the same truth.

John Milton wrote: *"The mind is its own place, and in itself can make a heaven of hell, a hell of heaven."*

Perspective became the doorway. Even in pain, the way we think becomes our world we live in. This is how powerful our minds are. Circumstances do not create our reality. Our perception does.

Modern Echoes

By the modern age, the message had become a call.

James Allen: *"As a man thinketh in his heart, so is he."*

Napoleon Hill: *"Whatever the mind can conceive and believe, it can achieve."*

Norman Vincent Peale: *"Change your thoughts and you change your world."*

Even as wars raged and fear loomed, truth was spoken like a compass pointing home.

Born of Suffering

In one of humanity's darkest hours, voices emerged like light.

Anne Frank: *"I don't think of all the misery, but of the beauty that still remains."*

Harriet Tubman: *"Every great dream begins with a dreamer… you have within you the strength, the patience, and the passion to reach for the stars to change the world."*

Helen Keller: *"Although the world is full of suffering, it is also full of the overcoming of it."*

Viktor Frankl: *"When we are no longer able to change a situation, we are challenged to change ourselves."*

Elie Wiesel: *"Even in darkness, it is possible to create light and encourage compassion."*

Nelson Mandela: *"I learned that courage was not the absence of fear, but the triumph over it."*

These voices came from those who had every reason to despair. Yet they chose to rise - and because of that, their wisdom still carries us.

The Living Thread Continues

In our own time, the same gentle truth calls us back.

Wayne Dyer: *"Change the way you look at things, and the things you look at change."*

Louise Hay: *"Every thought we think is creating our future."*

Maya Angelou: *"You may not control all the events that happen to you, but you can decide not to be reduced by them."*

Their words remind us: we are not victims of circumstance. We are creators of meaning. The choice is ours - suffering or freedom - and the decision begins with inner wisdom and directing thought. This is empowering.

The Living Truth

Confucius: *"The more man meditates upon good thoughts, the better will be his world and the world at large."*

Gandhi: *"Strength does not come from physical capacity. It comes from an indomitable will."*

Corrie ten Boom: *"Happiness isn't something that depends on our surroundings... it's something we make inside ourselves."*

Churchill: *"Attitude is a little thing that makes a big difference."*

The thread is unbroken. From ancient wisdom to modern voices, from those in peace to those in chains, the message is the same: Circumstances may cause suffering, but they do not need to become our home. The body may be caged, but the 'heart centred mind' (Agape) holds the key to our freedom. When it is aligned with wisdom, you are free indeed. Within that freedom lies the seed of transformation.

Seeing With Clarity

The Agape Bloom is not about avoiding the human experience - it is about seeing it with absolute clarity. It does not deny pain. It does not force the mind to feel "better."

It does not offer positivity, but a greater *truth* through the lens of *Agape*. Where toxic positivity tries to *mask* emotion (feelings are valid, just not a reliable guide to truth). Agape honors emotion - and removes the illusion that it defines or guides us to greater freedom.

It is not what trained psychologists know as *bypass*. Bypass reinforces fear by refusing to look at it. Agape dissolves fear by seeing it without judgement. It is the foundation of self compassion.

It does not dismiss trauma. It gently reminds us of presence and self connection through love.

It does not offer comfort as an escape route - it returns us to the only place that is truly safe: the space before thought, where the nervous system is not under psychological threat.

Healing in Agape is not an achievement. It is the absence of resistance. It is the embrace of acceptance. A return to the peace beneath the chaos. This is not 'think positive.' This is *'see'* clearly. Reconnect to your inner truth. Learn that you *can* trust this.

The Agape Bloom is not for those seeking control - it is for those ready to *end* the war within. For those who are ready to experience *The Sacred Ceasefire Of The Mind.*

Neuroplasticity – Reshaping Our Brain

The brain is not fixed. It is alive - fluid, reshaping, becoming. Science calls this neuroplasticity, but in *The Agape Bloom,* we call it seeds of probability. Every thought, every feeling, every choice is a seed. What you water becomes the landscape of your mind.

Thought is *not* small. It is energy, and energy creates form. Thought is a powerful energetic force. When the mind is aligned with the wisdom of Agape - we reshape our world from the inside out. This, many call *manifestation.* First comes the alignment within.

When you choose love, kindness, and compassion toward yourself, or others, you are not being "soft." Neuroscience agrees you are literally shaping your brain and body toward strength.

Chemistry concurs: oxytocin and dopamine bloom when love, in the form of kindness, is chosen - it strengthens memory, creativity, and resilience.

When the mind dwells on anger, hate, separateness or fear - it floods the body with cortisol. Stress constricts, shrinks, and locks us into rigid grooves. The garden withers.

This book offers you the possibility to see thought for what it is, to *reconnect* with wisdom via intuition, and to know the difference. Head noise, or reliable guidance?

Living In Connection

Our bodies are made up of 50% - 65% water. Like water, you are never static. You can soften. You can adapt. You can flow into new shapes. Like a nurtured garden, you are not barren - only waiting for seeds of love, truth, peace, and joy to flourish. Energy responds to attention. Therefore attention, aligned with your original state of *unconditional love* before the ego was formed , creates harmony beyond measure.

This is the *heart* of The Agape Bloom: helping you remember that your inner truth is not determined by your past, your diagnosis, or the chaos of the world. It is shaped moment by moment, by what you choose to water.

The Nature of Agape

The Unseen Yet Undeniable

Humans trust invisible forces every day. No one has seen electricity, gravity, or magnetic fields - we see its effects - light, heat, movement, and data transfer.

The moon moves entire oceans without touching the water, without permission or visibility. Wifi, radio waves, and data - information is exchanged invisibly.

We trust it because it works, not because we can see it. As humans we organise our lives around these dominant fields.

Absence of visibility has never been the absence of reality.

Love Is Not Passive

Love has been distorted into sentiment, reduced to feeling. Moreover, packaged as positivity. Because of this many dismiss it as naive, indulgent or emotional.

Love is not a mood nor an emotional preference. It has often been misused as a spiritual bypass - a way to avoid truth rather than live from it.

However - Agape is not avoidance. It is a *transformative healing energy.* We do not question the forces of electricity and gravity because we live by their effects.

Love belongs to this same category of reality. It is known not by appearance but by its impact. Where love is present, systems organise - where absent systems fragment.

What we often call 'mental illness' is the seen impact of whether love (safety, belonging and attunement) has been present or withdrawn.

Love here is not romance - it is coherence. Integration. A powerful force - unseen to the human eye, however seen by what it restores, regulates, and holds together.

We can clearly see the cumulative effects of its absence within the world every day and throughout history.

Humans are disconnected and suffering.

At the core of who we are - before the noise of the world settles in - There is peace. There is love. There is presence.

These are not things to chase or earn; they are our spiritual blueprint. Yet as life unfolds, our perceived self (ego) and fear-based survival, develops at astounding speed and momentum. We learn to measure, compare, and strive. We adopt stories of being broken, too much, or not enough - and mistake them for truth.

However, peace never leaves. It's simply buried beneath the noise. The moment we notice the racing of our minds - the swirl of what-ifs and judgments - that 'noticing' is already the beginning of return to our heart centre, our place of peace.

Letting go is not a battle; it is an intentional release. When we stop taking things personally, because we know the truth - our judgement of others and self, softens. The ability to choose compassion and understanding becomes an option. We find we have a greater choice over what we rest in and what we let go of.

From this place of quiet confidence, we remember that beneath the noise, we are whole, already connected to the gentle wisdom and truth within.

To live *truthfully* and aligned to the steady rhythm of *agape* is to honour the intelligence that shaped us.

The Nature Of Truth

'Truth' Appears Multi-layered.

Objective truth is steady and factual - the sun rises, the heart beats.

Subjective truth is how life feels from within - shaped by experience and perception.

Relational truth is truth in motion - honesty, integrity, and compassion expressed in daily life to self and others.

Spiritual truth is what remains when all stories fade: the awareness behind thought, the peace beneath emotion. It is unchangeable. Immovable. The highest, most reliable truth.

Agape Unites All.

It reminds us that everything is supported - even that, which we do not understand, or find difficult to accept - with our minds. Wisdom speaks clearly.

If thought *reduces* you, it's **not** aligned with the highest *truth*. This comes from subjective truth - shaped by experience and perception.

If thought *expands* you - bringing calm, curiosity, openess, compassion, understanding, and clarity - it carries spiritual truth within it. It is worthy of our attention.

Truth without love becomes judgment; love without truth becomes blind.

Together, they form *wisdom* - the kind that sees clearly and still chooses compassion - for self and others. Intuition is the *voice of wisdom*. Without a calm receptive system, we miss its gentle guidance.

Truth Is Not Fragmented

However - *our* perception is. Spiritual truth is whole. We do not usually meet it all at once. We first meet this fragmented version through the filter of our wounds, our conditioning, our culture, and our survival patterns. So, truth *appears* multifaceted - not because there are many truths - but because there are many levels of seeing.

The Three Layers of Truth

Personal Truth - "What I honestly feel right now."

This is deeply human and valid. It is shaped by your nervous system, past and current experiences, fears, and hopes. It is the echo of thought.
It is not necessarily always accurate compared to a broader perspective - but it is real to the one experiencing it.
This is where most conflict between people lives.

Collective Truth - "What *we* agree is real."

This is science, law, culture, religion, psychology.
It shifts as humanity evolves or new information is presented.
It can be more stable than personal truth - but still not the ultimate ground.

It is not affected by belief or agreement. It does not argue, defend, or persuade. It is what remains when egostistic illusion falls away - love, oneness, peace, understanding.

This is the realm of *higher consciousness*. This is where suffering dissolves.

The Gift of Knowing This

We do not need to *force* anyone into one viewpoint. We simply need to recognise which layer we (or they) are speaking from.

The arguments dissolve. The urgency softens. Compassion becomes possible. Important decisions based on clarity can be determined without confusion or doubt.

When we see with clarity through wisdom, we become more curious in understanding another rather than fixed in our *opinion*, which often leads to a stalemate in relationships. This usually results in both parties feeling unseen, unheard, and *wrong* in the eyes of another. Consequently - we further cement ourselves in our fixed views, causing even greater separation.

This is ego at play. This creates the *them/us* point of separation. Historical, and current conflict between human beings - resulting often in senseless wars is created by this ego driven fixed viewpoint of separation.

Wisdom enables us to see differently - more expansively, therefore reconnection becomes possible. We seek to understand rather than hold onto our ego driven line in the sand.

Humility is the softening that makes this possible - the willingness to admit we do not see the whole picture, to release the need to be right, superior or defended.

In humility, the heart listens before the mind concludes and understanding becomes an act of love rather than the need for control over outcomes.

We cannot point weapons at another when we see them as equally deserving of being loved, heard and valued. This understanding can be used when seeking harmony and connection instead of being *right*.

When the mind surrenders to the wisdom of the heart - *where truth does not change* - we have the capacity for reconnection and peace.

The Sacred Ceasefire Of The Mind

A pulse beneath the noise - where truth and love breathe as one. They are not separate paths but two expressions of the same divine intelligence, forever entwined like roots and sunlight, soil and rain.

Truth is the foundation, the still point - what remains when the mind's illusions fall away. It is the unwavering essence of what is real. *Love* is the movement - the breath through all things. It is truth in motion, the living energy that animates, connects, and heals.

One without the other loses its way. Truth without love hardens into judgment. It can cut, divide, and blind itself to its own indifference - rigid, cold, a sword without compassion.

Love without truth can dissolve into confusion. It clings, overextends, and forgets its integrity - it can become blind, enabling, and self-deceptive.

However, when truth and love unite - a higher coherence emerges - a flow of spiritual integrity. Stillness married to warmth. Clarity infused with compassion.

This is *Agape* - the union of higher consciousness. It is every single human being's blueprint and birthright. Truth has been distorted throughout history - perhaps innocently at times, by hierarchical religious teachings that confuse, block, and thwart the essence and flow of Agape and truth - often for personal or collective gain, to the detriment of the masses.

The Sacred Ceasefire of the Mind is when our fractured mind - (fixed in perception, pride, ego, misguided and misaligned justification) - finally accepts *the sacred ceasefire* as a higher truth. It bypasses the human mind and its complexities. It begins to trust the inner wisdom of the heart.

Agape Love & Truth are trustworthy, elemental, and born of simplicity. It is *life* calling us back to *who we are* beneath the noise, the chaos, & distraction. A return to wholeness - before the shaping of our personal 'identity' or personality. (ego)

When we operate from our higher consciousness, we no longer search for truth 'out there' or validation from others. We are secure - we see with clarity and operate from understanding.

We become the home of peace and wisdom.

Harmony from within flows outward, watering the sacred soil of self and others. Its seed begins in the heart of the individual.

Our words soften. Our perception sharpens. And we move differently through the world - not to fix or control, but to witness, to allow, to flow. To seek understanding - and speak clearly without confusion.

This is the bloom of higher consciousness.

When the mind rests in truth, the heart opens in love. When both align, the beginning of freedom activates - effortless, whole, sustainable, joyful.

Every living organism longs to grow and express its full blueprinted potential. When we stop clinging to control, ego-driven thought and justification - when we return to this original blueprint - we are *home*. We are *free*.

There is nothing that compares to this *peace*, which goes beyond any human comprehension. This is the inner transformation that reconnects us to *all that is*. This is the only way toward unity and peace with all humans despite historical unrest, division and hatred. There is a way forward.

The Nature of Simplicity

Not because simplicity is lost - but because we have lost the art of slowing down.

The world moves faster than the human heart was ever designed to beat.
We wake to noise, end our days with screens, and wonder why peace feels like a stranger. We determine success by how busy and productive we have become. We measure it by material accumulation and bank balances. We have missed the mark.

Simplicity is not a luxury of the past. It is a necessity of the soul.
It is how we return to what is real, what is true, and what is already within us.

A Century of Acceleration

A hundred years ago, life moved in rhythm with the body, the sun, the soil, and the seasons. Now it moves in rhythm with algorithms.

Sociologists call this social acceleration - a constant speeding-up of work, communication, and expectation. The faster we go, the more disconnected we become. We have replaced pauses with social notification pings, reflection with reaction. We are superficially connected to more people than ever, yet lacking in presence with them. Humans are disconnected and suffering.

We know everything about the world and almost nothing about ourselves.
We scroll through beauty, but rarely *feel* it. We speak endlessly, but listen scarcely.

Also still, a quiet knowing remains: this pace is unsustainable. This is not our natural state.

The Way Back to Simplicity

The Agape Bloom can help us remember what the modern world forgets - that truth is simple, and peace begins where mental, physical, and emotional clutter ends.

Simplicity is the catalyst to connection: to self, to others, to love itself. When we strip away noise, we create the space for life to speak again. When we create mental space, we shift from the mind's analysis to the heart's awareness. We begin to move from peace instead of over-thinking. We reconnect not through intellect, but authentically through wholeness and essence.

Simplicity doesn't come from force or strategy - it blooms naturally when we stop performing and start *be*ing.

Food - Returning to the Earth

True nourishment is simple. Whole Foods. Clean water. Gratitude for what we have. When we eat slowly, consciously, with reverence, we digest not only food but peace.
The act of preparing a meal becomes meditation - a quiet offering to the body that carries us.
Food that comes from the earth reminds us that healing begins with presence and patience. Every meal can be a prayer of return.

Environment - The Fire Test

If everything you owned disappeared in flames tonight, what would you miss the most?

Simplicity of environment asks us: What truly matters if all else is gone? When we clear physical space, we clear emotional and spiritual space too.

We make room for authentic expression, beauty, and meaning. Your home does not need to impress - it needs to express. Let it mirror your heart: uncluttered, peaceful, alive, expressive.

Connection — The Currency of Presence

Connection cannot be rushed. It thrives in the slow moments - in listening, in laughter, in silence shared. Presence is love's native language. When we simplify our attention, we deepen our relationships. When we stop rushing, we start seeing more clearly.

Connection is not built from intellect or performance, but from being rooted in the heart, unguarded and real. This is where empathy blossoms. This is where Agape thrives.

Work — The Trade of Time

We trade our hours for income, yet rarely question the cost. We work harder to afford more, to maintain more, to escape less. And still, peace slips further away.

Simplicity in work is about realignment - asking, *"what am I truly working for?"*

If it is freedom, connection, or meaning, then the way back is not more striving, but more truth. A slower pace is not laziness; it is wisdom. Time is the one currency that cannot be earned back. Spend it on what lights you up. Spend it on meaningful moments.

Simplicity as the Catalyst

Simplicity is the bridge between disconnection and devotion. It is how we come home - not just to our values, but to our *being*. When we simplify our lives and surroundings, we create space for new and fresh discovery. When we quiet the mind, we are essentially expanding our awareness for greater understanding.

Simplicity brings coherence between all parts of us - mind, body, and spirit. It returns us to our natural intelligence: *the wisdom of the heart.* In that space, self-connection is no longer a practice - it's a state of *Being.*

The Irony of "More"

Consumerism tells us that the answer lies in accumulation. But accumulation breeds anxiety. The

more we have, the more we manage. The more we manage, the more we lose sight of what matters. We have confused comfort with peace, and pleasure with fulfillment. Simplicity restores the distinction.
It reintroduces us to joy without excess, meaning without noise, and love without condition.

Simplicity as Truth

Simplicity is not emptiness; it is clarity. It is what remains when illusion and distraction are seen clearly.
It is what the soul has known all along: that peace is not found in what we *add*, but in what we let *fall away*. The things, people and beliefs that do not enrich the soil of our life.

Truth is not complex. It is quiet, steady, and waiting. And when we return to it, we realise we were never disconnected. Only distracted.

The Bloom of Enough

You were never meant to keep up with the world.
You were meant to be in rhythm with life.
The breath. The sunrise. The steady beat of the heart.

When you live simply, you live in harmony.
You return to love, to truth, to self, to others.
You become the space through which peace can flow.

Simplicity is not a trend.
It is a remembrance.
It is the soil of connection.
It is the quiet bloom of enough.

Part IV

The Field Of Harmony

Harmony Within

Personal boundaries are not fences we build to keep others out. They are the steady expression of clarity within - a compass that tells us when something aligns with who we are, and when it does not.

Here's a simple truth: if we don't know ourselves, if we haven't paid attention to what restores us and what drains us, what feels nourishing and what depletes us, then boundaries are shaky and unconvincing. How can we protect what we have not yet identified?

The starting point here is clarity. Clarity arises when we reconnect with our authentic truth, when we quiet the noise of thought long enough to sense what is real in our body, our heart, and our mind. From this place, boundaries no longer feel like rules to be set or defended.

They are natural, effortless expressions of knowing. We simply recognise: *"This doesn't belong here,"* or *"This feels right for me,"* and truth is verbalised without guilt or doubt.

The Agape Bloom is about personal reconnection to love & truth. We cannot live peacefully with self or others if we are strangers to ourselves. When we attune to all of our parts - intuition, senses, mind, body, and the wisdom of our heart - harmony returns. Confusion dissolves. What remains is simple and clear: who we are, what we value, and what no longer needs to be carried, or given attention to.

As our minds quieten, as our nervous systems heal, inner *knowing* expands and clarity emerges from this natural state. And from clarity, boundaries are no longer battles. They are simply our truth lived out loud, unapologetically.

The Inner Gauge

Think of your boundary as a finely tuned instrument. It hums when you are in alignment and sharpens the moment you betray yourself with a swallowed "no" or a forced "yes." Most of us were trained to ignore this inner gauge. We learned to please, to keep the peace, to avoid conflict. Over time, the instrument grew faint. But it never disappeared. With practice, you can hear it again.

Clarity Before Communication

Many believe boundaries are about what we say - a "no," a line drawn, a confrontation. But the deeper work comes first: clarity within.

When you are clear, your words become simple, powerful, and kind. We do not *wobble*. Or doubt. We do not over-explain. They sound like: "No, that doesn't work for me." or "I can't do that right now." "That's not something I choose." Short. Clear. Kind. And unwavering - because they rise from truth, not fear.

When The Line Is Crossed

With clarity, you don't need to live on guard. You can stay open, soft, and receptive. Because you trust that when a line is crossed, you'll know it - and you'll name it.

It might sound like: "I feel uncomfortable with how you're speaking to me." or "I need this conversation to pause." Again - "I don't share that opinion, and I won't continue this discussion."

This is not a drama. It is not a battle. It is simply honouring your compass, pointing you back to truth.

Why Boundaries Matter for Peace

Boundaries are not selfish. They are self-honouring. Without them, resentment grows and life becomes a performance for others. With them, balance returns. Space opens.

Paradoxically, boundaries don't push people away - they draw us closer to those we love more authentically. When others know where we stand, honesty replaces confusion. Real connection begins.

Listen inward: Notice when your body says *"no"* but your words say *"yes."*

Define one clarity: Name one thing that drains you. Acknowledge it.

. Practice one response: Create a short, kind phrase you can use. *"I can't take that on." "That doesn't feel right for me."*

Observe: Notice how you feel afterward. Lighter? More yourself? That is your compass confirming you are on track. If you *feel* slight guilt - that is only thought - and feeling is its echo. Trust your *'knowing.'*

Boundaries, at their heart, are not about controlling others. They are about protecting your own wholeness. When you know yourself fully, boundaries

95

stop being something you *set* - they become something you *live*.

And from that place, peace is no longer fragile or fleeting. It becomes the natural soil your life grows from.

The Continual Bloom

In every personal journey, we arrive at a point, where we must stop looking outside ourselves. Not because the world has nothing to offer - but because nothing outside us can give what we long for most.

The centre of you has been there all along. Quiet. Steady. Like a river running beneath the noise, like gold lying undiscovered - buried beneath the rubble.

When we are burnt out, overwhelmed, and dysregulated, the mental and emotional noise drowns this truth out. We can't hear it. We mistake the chatter for truth, the busyness for purpose, the exhaustion for weakness.

Here is the truth.

Your wisdom has never left you. Your intuition has never stopped speaking. It is simply waiting for the mind to soften, for the storm to pass, for you to remember where home is. Every principle in this book, I've shared, is not the power itself. It is a seed of understanding - and when accepted and nurtured it will lead you to your authentic original blueprint. This is an *inner* journey of the heart. The real experience begins not with practice, but with reconnection. The Agape Bloom insight is recognised by the heart, *not* understood with the mind .

Trusting that the quiet voice within you is not foolish, that your body, heart, & spirit know the way. Trusting that when the chatter falls silent, what remains is truth. You do not need to strive for it.

Neither, do you need to prove yourself worthy of it. You only need to see it. To allow yourself to rest in it. This is the great *reconnection* - wholly integrated into immovable, unconditional love and truth.

From this wholeness the following gifts feature in your life. This reconnection *is* the most restorative and peaceful journey you will experience.

Many cultures throughout the history of man have called this *Reconnection* many things - Higher Consciousness, God, Energy, Source, Creator, Providence, The Essence Within - these are just names, born of a human desire to label things we do not understand. To put into a convenient box - to describe the *indescribable*. The *I AM*, - the breath, the cosmos, the flower, the tree. Experiment - *play* - trust your guidance. Ask *Intuition* direct questions. Await the answer. This is your gift. And it is deeply personal.

This is *your* time to express authentically who you are - to colour this world with beauty, freedom, hope and joy. This is your personal invitation to fully *bloom*.

* See Appendix B, C and D - Intuition Reconnection Guides

The Gifts That Keep On Giving

Joy

Joy is not excitement or elevation. It is a settled sense of being at home within oneself - an anchored wellness that arises when we are no longer at war within. It flows from connection, not circumstance. Joy is the warmth that fills the space created from a peaceful and quietened mind.

Trust

Trust begins inward, in the unseen soil of self-agreement. Before ease with others, there must be safety within your own being. A body that no longer betrays itself to please. A heart that no longer silences truth to keep the peace. A mind that stops treating intuition as a threat. Trust in others is projection; trust in self is liberation. When self-trust returns, life simplifies. Boundaries are steady. Decisions clarify. The first bloom is always within.

Wholeness

Wholeness is not becoming more. It is remembering nothing was missing. Not improvement, but return. Not an achievement, but a reunion. Healing does not change who you are, it reveals your true essence; it gathers all of you back into one place. Nothing is pushed away. Everything is integrated with love. You were never broken. Only forgotten. This is the return to your whole self.

Freedom

Freedom is not escape from life, but release from inner captivity. It is the peace of no longer being ruled by fear. It is not an escape, but homecoming. We are not imprisoned by life, but by old stories and survival conditioning. Safety does not need to be earned. Love does not need to be proven. Freedom is not the absence of discomfort; it is the absence of self-abandonment. Like the sunflower, freedom comes from *knowing* its design and purpose, not striving. Quiet. Undramatic. Unapologetically present. You were never meant to live in survival. You are here to bloom to your greatest potential.

Peace

Peace is the absence of resistance. It is not fragile or fleeting, nor something to manage. Peace is presence - untouched by circumstance, history, or expectation. The mind seeks peace through control; the heart finds peace through trust. When thought loosens, peace arises naturally. It holds experience without becoming its identity. It does not erase pain; it simply does not *become* it. Peace is not a destination. It is your original state. Your birthright. Your truest nature.

Love

Love is the lens through which all of this becomes visible. It is not approval, agreement, or self-sacrifice. Love softens judgment and makes compassion possible - for ourselves and for others. It allows us to witness pain, difference, and behaviour without hardening or turning away. Love does not excuse harm, but it refuses to reduce a person to it. When we meet ourselves with love, shame loosens its grip. We release the need for approval and stop performing for belonging. Love restores dignity without demand. It becomes the bridge - not by forcing unity, but by remembering our shared humanity. Love does not need permission. It does not need to be earned. In its steady presence, separation heals and truth can breathe.

Seeds Of You

You have carried much, beloved one.

Too much.

Soil that was never yours,

storms that threatened your resilience.

And still - you grew.

Now you know the truth:

you *were never broken,*

never fragile,

never less than whole.

Even in the hardest soil,

the seed of light was within you.

May you stand tall like the sunflower,

face open to the dawn,

roots deep in the earth.

May you release what was never yours,

and rest in what always was.

Peace does not live in the future.

It is here.

Love does not come from chasing.

It is within.

And you, dear one,

are not a sponge but a bloom.

Go gently.

Plant and nurture your seeds of wisdom.

Shine without effort.

And remember:

coming home to yourself

is the greatest healing of all.

Part V

Closing

Seeds of Renewal

The sunflower's life does not end with the bloom. When golden petals fall, the center remains - full, heavy, abundant with seeds. Each seed carries potential for new life.

Some of her seeds nourish birds and other living creatures, including humans. Other seeds enrich the soil. Still others scatter on the wind to grow again.

The gift of the sunflower is not only its beauty while standing tall, but in what it leaves behind: nourishment, renewal, and future fields of bloom.

The journey of the sufferer follows the same pattern. Exhausted, bent, and carrying burdens that were never theirs, they now stand whole. They stand amongst their own kind. They stand tall and true to their purpose.

Their presence becomes nourishment. Their story becomes seed. Without absorbing or rescuing, they naturally inspire others - simply by living their truth.

Science

In biology, this is called the *cycle of regeneration.* The sunflower completes one life, but in doing so, it ensures the flourishing of many more.

In psychology, it is called *post-traumatic growth.* What we once believed would destroy us becomes the soil for wisdom, compassion, and deeper connection. The healed sufferer no longer seeks to fix everyone - or themselves. Instead, they stand rooted in authenticity, and that alone plants seeds of freedom in others.

Reflective Practices

- **Journaling Prompt:** What seeds do I want to plant in others through my healing? What qualities, stories, or truths do I wish to leave behind?

- **Letter to Self:** Write a note to your younger self, beginning with: Here is what I've learned… Let your words flow as a gift to the version of you who first bent under the weight of heaviness.

- **Now - Letter to Self:** Write a note to your future self, one year from today. Let your words be heart lead. From the place of wholeness and how your life has transformed through self compassion (Agape love) and truth.

- **Mini Ritual:** Hold a sunflower seed in your palm (or draw one on paper). Bless it as a symbol of what you will grow next - in yourself, and in the world. Whisper: From my healing, new life begins.

A Seed Of Agape

Your bloom was never just for you. Your healing ripples outward. Every truth you embody becomes a seed in the heart of another. Therefore the field grows - one sunflower becoming many.

Epilogue

Do I still dance the *quick step* with old patterns? Of course. *smiling to myself

I still get caught up in the mind's noise, still feel the sting of judgment and shame - from myself and others. But I no longer suffer as I used to. Now, *I know*. I know *who* I am and how to return to peace and self compassion. It takes as long as I choose. The power of choice is a wonderful gift.

What once took weeks, even months of suffering now takes hours, sometimes only minutes. I see the illusion. I see the habit. And I come *home* sooner, softer, kinder, clearer. Then…as *'life'* does - it likes to test us, to remind us how far we've come.

Not so long ago, an ongoing toxic workplace environment tested me deeply. With over five years of absence of debilitating depression and anxiety, I began to experience a familiar unease. I sought professional help, and it was clear it was situational anxiety. What this meant was anyone in this situation would have responded similarly. Looking back, I see that I made it through with greater strength than I realized at the time.

What would've once set me back into turmoil, depression, and self loathing for months, possibly years - was resolved reasonably quickly in comparison. Out of that triggering season, this unfinished book was inspired into completion.

After sitting untouched for two years as scattered ink in my journals, it came alive. I leaned into wisdom and clarity through that difficult period. Eighty percent of this book poured out of me in one month.

The Agape Bloom meets us at every turn. It's not about perfection - or freedom from painful life events. It's how we choose to respond. It is how we get back up. It is how we love ourselves through difficulties. It is freedom from *unnecessary* self-perpetuated suffering.

As former sufferers, we will never forget the years stolen through our innocence. We will never forget the injustices against us that shaped our thoughts, beliefs, and nervous system.

However, it is possible that we see those 'episodes' from an entirely new perspective. They no longer have life-long prison sentences. They were events outside our control. They belong exactly where they arrived. In the past. They can serve as a transformative springboard. We value our freedom. We choose our peace. We choose our battles.

We will never forget the ones we have loved and lost through personal battles of addiction and suicide. We remember how precious life is and how we are solely 100% responsible for our 'return to truth and peace'.

No one can rescue us from our suffering. This is an *inside* job. Only we, the individual - holds the key to freedom - we just need to realise it.

What we do forget, in time, is the disruption of 'accusatory thought' banging at the door of our mind. A new tenant resides there. Their name is Peace.

When the familiars come knocking - they never stay for long. As they leave, you can hear them mumbling how boring Peace is and how they don't feel welcome any longer. (although a funny little tale - it's actually correct)

Once we see this, accusatory thought no longer holds the power. We simply *know* the truth. We don't need to engage, pay attention, or justify. We realise it disappears as quickly as it arrives. No fuel - no fire.

A Seed Of Agape

When the mind surrenders to the heart, we bloom.

When the heart opens in love, truth reveals itself without effort.

In this elegant dance, love and truth are one - the doorway to higher consciousness - the remembrance that to know truth, is to be love, and to be love is to live in truth.

Seasons Of Bloom

You are not the end of the story,
you are the breath between its lines.
The pause between petal and sunlight,
between heartbeat and belonging.

Love did not begin with you,
and it will not end when you forget it.
It moves through every cell, every memory,
every whisper of your becoming.

You are not here to perfect the world.
You are here to experience it
to see the divine pulse in all its imperfect beauty,
to meet fear with gentleness, to meet life as a friend.

There will be seasons of opening,
and seasons of rest. Both are sacred. Both are love.

When you lose your way,
listen to the ancient pulse beneath the noise.
It is the same song that called the stars awake,
the same one that beats in your chest.

It will guide you back - to stillness, to truth,
to the heart that never closed.

For the bloom never ends.
It only deepens. And you -
you are part of its unfolding.

Appendices

Prolonged Chronic Stress

Our typically understood 'six senses' are not just how we experience life - they are how the body remembers safety.

Before the mind creates stories, before anxiety tightens the chest, the body scans the world through sensation: the warmth on your skin, the softness of breath, the subtle scent of the morning air. When we spend too long in stress or hypervigilance, those senses become distorted - the world feels too loud, too fast, too unsafe. The gut can become inflamed. Digestion freezes. The body no longer feels like home.

Self Compassion ~ The Balm For Our Senses

The quiet taste of real food.
The texture of sunlight on skin.

The scent of rain.

The sound beneath the noise.

The simple miracle of breath moving through the ribs.

These are not small things.

They are the nervous system's proof that we are safe again.

They are how the gut begins to awaken and trust.

They are the doorway back to regulation, to truth, and peace.

How It Shapes Our Senses

Prolonged stress doesn't only weigh on the mind. It reshapes how we experience the world through every sense. Sight, sound, touch, taste, smell, even intuition - all become distorted when the nervous system is in survival. What was once a way of connecting to life's beauty becomes a filter for threat.

Sight (Vision)

Stress sharpens the eyes for danger. The sympathetic nervous system dilates the pupils and narrows peripheral vision, producing tunnel vision. We scan for what is wrong, overlooking what is safe or beautiful. Over time, this wiring becomes a habit - the brain sees danger even in stillness. Migraines, eye strain, and blurred vision often follow as cortisol and muscle tension accumulate.

Sound (Hearing)

The stressed nervous system tunes itself to survive. This makes the ears hypersensitive to sharp or sudden sounds, a trait called **hyperacusis**. Even ordinary noises feel unbearable. The startle reflex heightens, and the brain struggles to filter background noise. Crowded rooms can feel chaotic, even painful.

Touch (Somatic Sensation)

Flooded with stress hormones, the body braces. Muscles hold tension, skin grows sensitive, and chronic pain may develop. Conditions like fibromyalgia and IBS often link back to prolonged stress and nervous system dysregulation. For sensitized people, touch can swing - sometimes craving comfort, other times recoiling as if every sensation is too much.

Taste

Stress disrupts the gut microbiome, and the gut directly shapes taste. Cortisol reduces saliva, dulling flavors. Food becomes flat, or cravings surge for sugar and salt - the body's quick route to dopamine. The vagus nerve's disrupted signals can lead to emotional eating or loss of appetite. Eating loses its pleasure, becoming a way to numb rather than nourish.

Smell

Smell connects directly to memory and emotion through the limbic system. Under stress, the nose sharpens toward danger - smoke, chemical odors - but dulls toward pleasure. Over time, cortisol can blunt the olfactory bulb, muting smell. Joy is lost in this dullness; the scent of flowers, bread, or a loved one's skin fades into the background.

Perhaps the deepest impact of stress lies here. Hypervigilance scrambles intuition. Instead of clear gut wisdom, the body signals fear: a racing chest, a knot in the stomach, thoughts looping in alarm. True intuition, which arises in calm, gets buried beneath noise. The sensitive sufferer is left second-guessing, doubting, chasing certainty.

Reconnecting To Heart Wisdom

(7 Visualisation Guides)

As we come to the close of *The Agape Bloom*, you may find that much of what you've read has resonated deeply - and yet a quiet uncertainty remains: *How do I actually connect with this place inside myself? How do I trust what I hear?*

This is natural.

Reconnection is not an act of effort. It is an act of trust.

These meditations are here to help you with that.

They are gentle, simple, five-minute invitations back into your own inner wisdom.

You may read them silently, read them aloud, record them and listen, or simply let their rhythm guide you into a softer space of being. The visualisations shared here are brief introductions. Extended, fully guided versions are available as free downloads at **theagapebloom.com**, should you prefer a longer, audio-led experience.

What matters is not the method - but that you slow down enough for the truth inside you to rise. Because intuition speaks quietly. Unlike thought, which leaps and predicts. Unlike feeling, which surges and fades - intuition is steady, grounded, unmistakable once you learn its language. It does not argue. It simply *knows*.

Within the closing of each meditation I encourage you to ask your intuition to speak to you - any question you would like answered. Have a pad and pen ready to write the answers.

There are no right or wrong answers. You will find intuition speaks plainly. Simply. Sometimes with imagery. Within the stillness, when our minds are quiet - we can connect deeply.

The messages will always be aligned with love and truth. If not - then this will be your thoughts. Learn to recognise when you feel a sense of *knowing*. Trust yourself.

These meditations are your space to explore, to play, to rediscover the gentle guidance beneath the noise. Don't be surprised if you discover a certain playfulness when you connect with your inner wisdom.

I have asked questions, during my Intuitive Journaling Sessions, and I'm pleasantly surprised when guidance given, is often playful in nature. These delightful experiences remind me how serious we become when we have lived in cycles of survival. We forgot lightheartedness and joy. Intensity took its place.

Let these meditations be your bridge back to the truest part of who you are: untouched by fear, guided by clarity - the part that has been waiting patiently for your return. This is the beginning of your reconnection and where trust grows. The safe place where you connect into your fullness.

The Sacred Ceasefire Of The Mind

When the Inner War Grows Quiet

Close your eyes…
and let a long, slow breath loosen the edges of your body.

For a moment, simply feel the ground holding you,
as if the earth itself is saying,
"You don't need to brace anymore."

There is a field within you
where the mind finally puts down its weapons,
its analysing, predicting, preparing, defending.
You can step into that field now.

Imagine dawn softening the horizon.
A pale golden light spreads slowly
across a quiet meadow.
This is the ceasefire.
This is the moment when nothing inside you
needs to chase safety.

Thoughts may flutter at the edges,
small birds unsure where to land.
Let them. You do not have to attend to them.
You can let them be the background.

Feel your breath deepen…
as if your ribs are remembering
how to open without fear.

In this gentle light,
notice beneath the mind's noise
a different texture,
something calm,
something ancient,
something that feels like home.

It is your intuition,
your inner knowing,
the quiet one who never left.

You do not have to silence the mind
to hear this deeper voice.
You only need to stop fighting it.

Let this truth rise softly:

**"When I stop warring with myself,
my wisdom returns to me."**

Rest in the stillness between thoughts.
Feel the quiet widen.
Feel the deeper knowing move toward you with ease.

You are reconnecting.

The Roots Of Agape

Take a gentle breath in… let it fall out like a leaf drifting to earth.

Imagine yourself walking into a wide field of sunflowers,
tall, golden, warm.
They do not try to be beautiful. They simply turn toward what is true.

Find one sunflower and sit beside it.
The ground beneath you is steady, solid as belonging.

Thoughts may whisper their familiar doubts.
Feelings may echo old memories.
Let them drift.
They do not understand Agape.

Agape is older than your wounds.
Older than your striving.

Older than every version of you that believed it had to earn love.

Imagine roots growing softly
from the base of your spine,
sliding down into the earth,
finding steadiness,
finding nourishment.

These roots carry a truth your mind cannot argue with:

"I am already held. Not because I proved anything, but because I exist."

Let your breath deepen.
Let warmth expand in your chest,
slowly, like sunrise, unhurried.

Feel that something ancient within you
is reconnecting to love
that never needed to be deserved.

This is the soil that nourishes you.
This is the love that steadies you.
This is the truth that has never once
turned away.

Rest here in the quiet, rooted, belonging.

The Trustworthy Guide

Dropping Beneath the Noise of the Mind

Close your eyes softly.
Let your breath fall into a natural rhythm,
as though your body remembers
how to breathe without trying.

In your mind's eye,
see yourself standing beside
a moving river.

Thoughts rush past
like fast water,
busy, dramatic, urgent.
Feelings rise and fall
like swirling currents,
intense, shifting, insistent.

You do not jump in.
You stay on the shore.
Close enough to witness,
far enough to remain untouched.

Let the river keep moving.
You are not here
to fix the water
or swim inside its stories.

Bring your awareness downward
below the noise
into the chest…
into the belly…
into a quiet place
just beneath the ribcage.

Place a hand there gently.

Imagine a small golden flame,
steady, unwavering,
unmoved by the river above.

This is where your intuition lives.
Not in the turbulence.
Not in the highs or lows.
But beneath them,
in the quiet,
in the clarity,
in space that does not react.

Let your breath nourish that flame.
Let it grow warmer, brighter,
more certain. And whisper inwardly:

**"Thoughts interpret.
Feelings react.
My intuition knows."**

Feel yourself resting
in a place deeper than thinking,
deeper than emotion,
a place that has been waiting
for your return.

Stay here for a moment.
Let the river move.
Let the wisdom remain.

You are reconnecting
to the truth beneath every storm.

The Sunflower Paradox

Imagine yourself as a young sunflower,
tender, curious, unsure.

In your youth, you bent restlessly
from east to west,
chasing the sun
as though it could leave you.

Feel that restlessness for a moment,
the scanning, the leaning, the seeking.

Now imagine yourself grown,
tall, golden, grounded.
You no longer chase light.
You receive it.

Place a hand over your chest.

Feel how much energy returns
when you stop scanning,
stop bending,
stop chasing.

Let this truth land gently:

**"What is meant for me is constant.
I do not have to pursue it."**

Feel the warmth of a steady sun
pouring over you,
effortless, generous, unwavering.

You are learning to trust the Source
instead of the search.

Rest in that warmth.
Let it teach your nervous system
what constancy feels like.

Truth As Stillness

The Quiet That Knows

Take a slow breath in…
and let the exhale soften your whole face.

Imagine entering a quiet room
with no windows, no noise, no clocks.
Only stillness,
the kind that feels like a warm blanket.

Sit in the centre of the room.

Thoughts arrive and fade
like dust in sunlight.
Feelings rise, then dissolve.

But beneath them,

beneath the movement,

is a deep, unmoving presence.

Truth. Not opinion. Not preference. No reaction.

Truth that simply **is**.

Imagine a single candle in the room,

its flame steady and untouched.

This flame represents truth.

Not loud.

Not dramatic.

Not emotional.

Just clear.

Breathe into that clarity and whisper:

"Stillness reveals what thinking cannot."

Rest in the quiet

that has always been known.

Fall Of The False Self

Close your eyes softly.

Imagine standing before a tall mirror -
but the reflection you see
is layered with old armour:
roles, expectations, fears, personas.

These layers were protection,
not identity.

Take a slow breath in…
and as you exhale,
a single layer softens and falls away.

The layer of pretending.
The layer of performing.
The layer of needing approval.

Breathe again. Slowly exhale …
Another layer dissolves.

The layer of self-doubt.
The layer of comparison.
The layer of striving.

One more breath & release
Another layer falls.

The layer that believed
you had to become something
to be enough.

Now look again.

What remains is simple,
your essence,
your truth,
your unprotected self.

Whisper gently:

"I am allowed to be who I am."

Rest in the freedom
of shedding what was never yours.

Whisper:

"I am allowed to be myself without armour."

Rest in your own soft authenticity.

Invitation:

Ask your intuition softly:
"Which layer of my false self am I ready to release next?"
Wait for the knowing.
Trust what rises.

Living From Alignment

The Quiet Yes of the Inner Compass

Close your eyes and breathe slowly.

Imagine a path lined with tall sunflowers
each one turning toward you
as you walk.

They do not judge your steps.
They simply reflect alignment.

Place a hand over your heart.

Feel the quiet pulse there -
steady, sure, ancient.

Imagine a soft golden thread
running from your heart
out into the horizon.

This thread represents alignment,
the path that feels like truth,
not effort.

Whenever you step away from it,
your body tightens.
Your breath shortens.
Your intuition dims.

Whenever you step toward it,
your body softens,
your breath steadies,
your *knowing* expands.

Take a breath and as you slowly exhale
feel yourself turn inwardly
toward what feels like a quiet yes.

A yes not from the mind.
A yes not from emotion.
A yes from inner truth.

Whisper: **"My life opens when I align,
not when I strive."**

Walk a few steps on this inner path,
soft, slow, guided.

You are reconnecting to the place
where wisdom leads
and peace follows.

Whisper:

"My life opens when I follow what feels aligned."

Walk inwardly toward that yes.

Sensory Reconnection Ideas

There is no 'requirement' for lengthy practices, modalities, or rituals here, though the following simple practices can assist us in getting present to the current moment through our senses.

What works for one may not work for another. This is your freedom, and your path to you. Get creative - have fun with this process.

As you become more familiar with peace and a quieter mind, you naturally begin to notice when you are off center. You will feel the contrast between being at *home* within yourself and being caught up in mental noise (distraction) which often shows up as unease in the body.

The following may assist you to reconnect more quickly to stillness if you find yourself struggling. It is *human* to get distracted and lose balance. The best part - when familiar, we notice it when it happens. We have found our new 'norm'. This is all part of our finding our true compass - from which everything else flows.

Candle Gaze - Watch a flame dance, steady and alive.

Color Hunt - Choose a color and notice it in five places.

Sunset Pause - Witness the sky shift without distraction.

Shadow Play - See shapes and stories in shadows.

Petal Study - Look closely at a flower, as if for the first time.

Morning Light - Watch daylight slowly enter your room.

Eye Yoga - Move your eyes in slow circles.

Photograph Joy - Capture something that makes you smile.

Mirror of Nature - Notice your reflection ripple in water.

Nature Choir - Step outside, hear the layers of sound.

Song Burst - Play one uplifting song, let it move you.

Humming Breath - Hum softly on each exhale.

Drumbeat - Tap a rhythm with your hands.

Silence Ritual - Sit quietly, listen to the depth.

Echo Game - Mimic a bird or nearby sound.

Voice Kindness - Record kind words to yourself, play them back.

Water Sound - Pour water slowly, listen closely.

Gratitude Whisper - Whisper three things you're thankful for.

Stone Hold - Feel the weight of a smooth stone.

Fabric Feel - Run fingers over different textures.

Hand Warmth - Rub palms together, place on your heart.

Barefoot Walk - Step onto grass, sand, or floor.

Warm Mug - Hold a warm drink, notice the heat.

Leaf Caress - Trace the veins of a leaf.

Hand Massage - Press each finger gently.

Pulse Feel - Rest fingers on your wrist, notice your heartbeat.

Water Splash - Splash cool water on your face.

Grounding Touch - Place both hands firmly on the earth.

Savor a Square - Let chocolate melt slowly on your tongue.

Fruit Meditation - Eat one berry with full attention.

Spice Sip - Sip warm water with ginger, cinnamon, or lemon.

Chew Slowly - Take one bite, chew twenty times.

Herbal Taste - Chew a sprig of mint or parsley.

Sour Awake - Taste lemon, notice your body's reaction.

Sweet Pause - Taste honey slowly.

Texture Test - Compare crunchy vs. soft foods.

Blind Taste - Close your eyes, taste something familiar.

Joyful Bite - Eat something playful, just for joy.

Flower Sniff - Inhale the scent of a bloom.

Coffee Aroma - Breathe deeply before sipping.

Herb Rub - Rub rosemary, basil, or mint between fingers.

Candle Breath - Smell a candle before lighting.

Spice Jar - Open a spice jar, inhale slowly.

Soap Ritual - Smell your favorite soap as you wash.

Fruit Peel - Peel citrus, inhale its zest.

Incense Pause - Light incense, notice the smoke.

Essential Oil - Place a drop on your wrist, inhale.

Book Smell - Smell the pages of a book.

Dream Note - Write one dream symbol, explore its meaning.

Silent Question - Ask inwardly, wait for the whisper.

Word Whisper - Let one word float up from your center, write it down.

Body Compass - Think of a pressing decision: does your body expand or contract with each answer?

First Thought - Record your first waking thought.

Color Sense - Ask, *"What color do I need today?"*

Intuitive Doodle - Draw freely, see what emerges.

Three Breaths - Take three slow breaths and exhales, listen inwardly.

A Seed Of Agape

Chronic stress narrows and hardens our senses. The world becomes sharper, harsher, dangerous and less alive. But this distortion is not permanent. As we align all parts of us, vision widens, sound softens, touch soothes, taste delights, smell comforts, and intuition reawakens as a steady compass. We now know we can trust our senses, intuition & inner guidance.

"When aligned, your senses are gateways back to yourself. Each small practice is a way of remembering: you are here, you are alive, and you are free to be reconnected fully."

Nature, Play & Joy

(5 min practices)

Play and presence are medicine for the nervous system. These practices are designed to cool the stress response, reconnect you with your senses, and remind you that joy is simple, accessible, and healing.

Why Play Matters

Play doesn't always come naturally to adults. Life gets serious, busy, full of responsibility - and somewhere along the way, we forget how to be lighthearted. We trade silliness for structure, curiosity for schedules.

But joy hasn't left you. It's still within, waiting for an invitation. Even the smallest act of play - twirling in the kitchen, blowing bubbles, laughing at something silly - soothes the nervous system. The body feels the difference. It whispers: *"I am safe. I can relax. I can breathe again."*

I had the privilege of becoming a young grandmother at the age of 49. My grandchildren taught me to be silly again - I'm affectionately called "Crazy Nana, Fun Nana & more recently Grumpy Nana"

Together, we dance, laugh, and create. Playfulness is presence. And I encourage you: give yourself permission to get your *silly* back. It's refreshing.

These rituals are not about perfection or performance. They are invitations - little doorways back to delight, to curiosity, to joy as medicine. At first, it may feel awkward. But awkward is simply the warm-up to joy.

Barefoot Walk - Step outside and walk barefoot on grass, sand, or soil. Notice the textures.

Tree Hug - Wrap your arms around a tree and feel its steady presence.

Petal Touch - Close your eyes and run your fingers gently over a flower petal.

Cloud Gaze - Lie down and watch clouds drift. Spot shapes and stories.

Water Play - Dip your hands in a stream, bucket, or bowl of water. Notice the coolness and flow.

Creative Play

Nature Collage - Gather three small items (leaf, stick, flower) and arrange them into a little artwork.

Stick Drawing - Use a stick to draw spirals, words, or doodles in dirt or sand.

Leaf Rub - Place a leaf under paper and rub over it with crayon or pencil. Watch the veins appear.

Rock Painting - Paint a small stone with bright colors or a word of hope.

Shadow Shapes - Use sunlight and leaves to trace shadows onto paper.

Sound & Movement

Birdsong Pause - Sit still and listen for bird calls. Try to mimic one softly.

Wind Dance - Stand outside, close your eyes, and sway with the breeze.

Bug Watch - Spend a few minutes following the tiny journey of an ant or bee.

Rustle Rhythm - Collect a few leaves and crunch them in your hands like an instrument.

Nature Breath - Breathe deeply with eyes closed, imagining you are inhaling the scent of trees or flowers.

Wonder & Imagination

Tiny Explorer - Pretend you are small, exploring the world at ground level. What do you see?

Name the Sky - Look up and give the sky a new name for the day.

Wish on the Breeze - Whisper a wish into the wind and imagine it being carried away.

Flower Friend - Pick one flower and imagine it has a personality. What would it say?

Stone Story - Hold a rock and imagine the journey it has been on for thousands of years.

10 More 'Just-for-Fun' Practices

Doodle Without Rules - Let your hand move freely across the page. No outcome, just flow.

Finger Paint - Smear colors with your hands. Enjoy the texture.

Dance Like Nobody's Watching - Play one joyful song and move however you like.

Bubble Play - Blow bubbles and watch them float, reflecting light.

Play Pretend - Turn an object into something else (a spoon becomes a microphone, a book a spell).

Make Shapes With Your Body - Stretch into letters, or become a tree, a star, a wave.

Hum or Sing Nonsense Sounds - Let silly syllables become a tune.

Chalk Art - Draw big, bold shapes on a footpath. Impermanent joy.

Five-Minute Lego Build - Stack blocks into a tiny sculpture.

Spin & Stop - Spin gently and notice where you land. Call it your "treasure spot."

Closing Reflection

Joy isn't a luxury. It's medicine. It's healing for your spirit. And it's always available - right here, at this moment. Give yourself permission to play. Then, create your own rituals and share them with others. Lightness spreads!

Nervous System/Gut Healing Food

Fifteen years ago - long before gut health was a "thing" I set myself an experiment. Curious about the Zero Waste movement, I decided to live one month without packaged products. Recyclable cardboard, tin, and glass - yes. Non recyclable packaging - no.

What I didn't expect was how my brain and gut would respond.

Without the processed packaged 'food' - without the preservatives, sugars, and additives - I was left with whole simple foods: vegetables, fruit, meat from the butcher in my own containers. I cooked everything from scratch.

Within weeks, I noticed something shifted. My brain fog lifted. My mind felt lighter, my body calmer. Nothing outside my life had changed - yet I was calmer, clearer in my thinking. I had been struggling with IBS for a number of years. This also improved significantly within the month.

I decided to do some more research. This was before 'Google search' became my friend. The local library was my main source of information.

I discovered the book *I Quit Sugar*, written by Australian journalist and TV host Sarah Wilson who was open about her bipolar disorder, who described how removing sugar assisted in stabilising her mental health. Much of her story mirrored my *'accidental discovery'*.

I had also witnessed this with my brother Stevie. Diagnosed with BPD, bipolar, anxiety, and depression at different times, he seemed to flourish, months at a time when he fueled his body well and stayed active.

Devastatingly, addiction pulled him in another direction. His story reminds me often how food and self-care matter.

I gently encourage you to test this for yourself, when you have the inclination. Notice how your body and mind respond. Do the research. Experiment gently. See what happens in your own body, and mind.

When we choose simplicity in any area of our lives, life improves. We begin to notice how much of our life - even our diets - have been shaped by outside voices telling us what is good, what is bad, what we must eat, what we must avoid.

Somewhere along the way, we lost our ability to *trust* ourselves. We leaned on *experts*, and forgot the quiet accountability of our own body and wisdom.

Coming back to wholeness means gently pulling back the curtain - seeing the difference between convenient truths and truth itself.

What we eat does more than fuel our bodies - it shapes how we feel, how we think, even how we meet the day. For years, I didn't realise this simple truth. Like many, I assumed low feeling was something I had no control over - a storm that arrived without warning. But food, it turns out, is one of the quiet levers we can lean on.

Research continues to confirm what intuition already knows: the closer our food is to its natural form, the kinder it is to both body and mind. Fruits, vegetables, wholegrains, legumes, nuts, seeds, organic meat - these are not just "healthy options," they are nature's original design, carrying the vitamins, minerals, and plant compounds our nervous system and brain quietly depends on.

This doesn't mean perfection. It doesn't mean never deviating from eating whole foods that nourish our gut and brain. The question to ask is simple: How close is this food to the way nature made it? The closer the answer, the more likely it is to steady your inner world.

Food as a Love Language

Every bite is more than calories - it is information. It tells your body whether you are safe, nourished, supported or whether it must brace for survival. So let food be a love language to yourself. Choose meals that create your *'calm'* rather than spike your stress. Notice how whole, simple foods bring clarity where brain fog once lived. Let eating become less about rules and more about kindness - a way of showing up for yourself, one plate at a time.

Your Body Is Not Betraying You - It's Asking for Help

If you find yourself anxious, easily fatigued, emotionally reactive, or caught in a fog of overwhelm, your body isn't betraying you. It may be undernourished. It may be asking for help. Your nervous system is not only wired - it is fueled. And what you fuel it with, *matters*.

The Missing Link

We often talk about healing through therapy, breathwork, boundaries, and self-inquiry.
But very few speak of the biochemical side of regulation.

When I was at my physical worst, (fibromyalgia, was the phantom guess by two different doctors when I sought help) there was little conversation about this link. And yet - our brain and body cannot function, let alone feel safe, without the right nutrients. Everything is connected.

This is not about diet culture or perfection. It's about supporting your biology so your gut and brain can do their job - producing the chemistry you need to feel clearer, calmer, and more alive. In the meantime, instead of removing everything at once, just begin simply by adding the following into one meal a day.

Nourishment for a Calm Nervous System

This section is an invitation, not a prescription. It is not a comprehensive guide to gut healing or nervous system support. Every body is different, and foods, herbs and supplements may interact with medications. Please research what is right for you and seek medical guidance where needed.

The nervous system does not respond to logic - it responds to care. Food is one of the simplest ways we communicate safety to the body. Not through rules or restriction, but through kindness.

Magnesium-Rich Foods

Relax the body, calm the mind, support sleep

Spinach, kale, pumpkin seeds, avocado, bananas, cacao (dark chocolate)

Healthy Fats (Omega-3s)

Feed the brain, reduce inflammation

Salmon, sardines, flaxseed, chia, walnuts, olive oil, eggs

Antioxidant-Rich Foods

Protect brain cells, reduce stress load

Blueberries, raspberries, beetroot, turmeric (with black pepper), leafy greens, green tea

High-Quality Proteins

Support serotonin and dopamine

Grass-fed meats, lentils, beans, quinoa, organic eggs, bone broth

Fermented & Gut-Loving Foods

Support the gut-brain connection

Sauerkraut, kimchi, kefir, miso, coconut yogurt, garlic, onion

- Refined sugar - blood sugar crashes feel like emotional chaos

- Excess caffeine - mimics anxiety and spikes cortisol

- Ultra-processed foods - inflame the gut and brain Alcohol - depletes nutrients and dulls emotional processing.

- This is not about control. It is about care. One loving bite at a time.

- Start the day with protein + healthy fat (e.g., eggs and avocado)

- Drink warm lemon water or herbal tea to ground

- Snack on nuts, seeds, or hummus with vegetables

- Include magnesium-rich foods at dinner to support sleep

- Eat slowly. Let meals become moments of presence

A Gentle Reminder

You do not need to change everything. Begin with one kind, intentional choice. Notice how your body responds. Let nourishment become an act of listening.

Because you didn't just eat. You showed up for yourself.

A Seed Of Agape

"When we begin to move toward kindness to self - we show up for ourselves like never before."

A Gift To Yourself

It is human to become desensitized to the wonder of life.

When we see delight shine in a child's eyes, as they see nature's beauty for the first time, it is one of the most joyful moments we can experience.

We lose this curiosity and presence as we get 'busy' and distracted with more '*important*' matters.

We miss the invitation of life itself.

Right now, at this moment - I invite you to read the following *slowly, intentionally*.

Through the gift of imagination, see through the eyes of a child, discovering something as if, for the first time.

You Are a One-Time Expression Of Life.

Every human fingerprint is unique - formed before birth, never to exist again. Even identical twins differ.

Within every cell, our genetic code carries subtle variations that make you singular in all of time.

You are a one-time expression of life.

Your essence, gifts, and voice are not accidents - they are necessary. They are uniquely yours. This is life's gift to *you*.

When we forget who we are, the world loses colour.

Authenticity is not rebellion; it is your gift of return to *life,* fully.

The Practice of Returning

When the mind begins to spiral, notice it, then pause.

Place your hand over your heart and whisper: *"I'm willing to see this through love. These thoughts are not truth."* Then breathe slowly in through your nose and exhale even more slowly through your mouth. Repeat this three times. Notice how your body softens.

That softening is truth returning - love dissolving illusion.

170

Reflection Prompts

1. What makes me uniquely me?

2. When do I feel most authentic and alive?

3. How does love shift the way I see myself and others?

4. What does truth feel like in my body?

5. How can I express the truth with more kindness and courage? To myself? To others?

Further Reading

Trauma / Boundaries / Authentic Healing

Maté, Gabor. *When the Body Says No: Exploring the Stress-Disease Connection.* Wiley, 2003.→

Maté shows how emotional suppression leads to physical illness.

Echoing *The Agape Blooms* principles that peace and authenticity protect the body.

Maté, Gabor. *In the Realm of Hungry Ghosts: Close Encounters with Addiction.* North Atlantic Books, 2008.

Explores compassion for the self through the lens of addiction. Deeply relevant to *The Agape Bloom's* concept of returning to wholeness.

van der Kolk, Bessel. *The Body Keeps the Score: Brain, Mind, and Body in the Healing of Trauma.* Penguin Books,

2015. Integrates neuroscience and somatic healing - grounding The Agape Bloom's reflections on how love and safety transform the nervous system.

Thought / Energy / Neuroplasticity

Dispenza, Joe. *Breaking the Habit of Being Yourself: How to Lose Your Mind and Create a New One*. Hay House, 2012.

Central to The Agape Blooms exploration of how thought forms energy. Dispenza bridges science and spirit, showing that transformation begins within.

Dispenza, Joe. *Becoming Supernatural: How Common People Are Doing the Uncommon*. Hay House, 2017.

Connects emotion, energy, and intention — reinforcing *The Agape Bloom's* principles of aligning thought and heart coherence.

The Three Principles / Mind–Spirit Connection

Banks, Sydney. *The Missing Link: Reflections on Philosophy and Spirit.* Lone Pine Publishing, 1998.

Explains the foundations of mind, consciousness, and thought - the framework that underpins *The Agape Blooms* view of inner peace as remembrance.

Banks, Sydney. *The Enlightened Gardener.* Lone Pine Publishing, 2001.

A narrative teaching of truth through parable, mirroring *The Agape Bloom's* poetic and allegorical tone.

Neill, Michael. *The Inside-Out Revolution: The Only Thing You Need to Know to Transform Your Life.* Hay House, 2013.

A modern interpretation of the Three Principles that complements *The Agape Blooms* simplified voice for readers seeking clarity.

Relationships

Lukeis, Fiona. *Funny Little Human: Transform The Way You See Yourself & The Ones You Love* Barnes & Noble 2025 - The Relatable Programme was the catalyst for the author's personal discovery and freedom. *The gift that keeps on giving.*

Acknowledgments

To My Cherished Seeds

Shannon, Daniel, Kelsey, and Tre - you are the reason I remained diligent in my search for freedom from invisible chains. You are in every page of this book - my heart is full of love and gratitude for each of you.

To my wonderful daughters-in-law - Alana and Hannah - I am grateful for our love and bonds. You have gifted me with so much individually and through our precious Israel, Isaac, Parker James, Luke & Loveia - and to our most recent additions - James and Emile. Thank you for enriching our family circle as it expands - as naturally as Agape does.

To My Family

Papa Bear - A survivor. A sufferer. By sheer grit and determination, you've carried yourself through years of discomfort and disconnection. You served in a senseless war and came home with invisible scars - yet you kept going. I see you, Dad. I love you.

Mumsie - Thank you for bringing the laughter out in Dad, for reminding us that joy is medicine too. You have a gift for gathering "homeless chicks" from all corners of the globe and creating family wherever you land. I'm so grateful for our custom-built tribe. Alannah - I miss you, you are seen. Shar - Baileys?

To My Beautiful Mother - You are still the most beautiful human I've known. The way you saw yourself was never true to how the world saw you. You were - and are - love in form. You taught me compassion, patience, forgiveness, and tenderness. You carried too much, but you did it with grace and kindness.

You once said, "Oh Lucy - don't be like me," when you realised I felt the world as deeply as you did. I *am* like you, Mum - and those are my favourite parts. I've just learned to balance the depth with agape & truth. I love you endlessly.

Michelle - Thank you for your love and loyalty through every version of me - the messy, the mending, and the blooming. Even when it was hard, we kept the door open. We've done well, sis. We chose connection over being right. Mum would be proud. I love you. Thanks to Jess, Shinaed, Summer, Keiana, and Ruku - thank you for being part of home away from home and for those chaotic, love-filled family gatherings. I miss that hub of laughter and noise. Great memories.

Brett - You are my brother, and I miss you. When we lost Darrin, then Stevie, it felt like you faded too. Please know you are loved - deeply, truly, unconditionally. You are worthy of truth and love. You are worthy to stand tall like the sunflower, drawing strength from Source. You are seen. You are heard. The bloom is available equally to all, especially the broken hearted.

I hope you get to read this book - it holds the seeds of our shared pain and the wings of our healing. You're part of my story, my roots, and my recovery. Your kindness during my darkest years will never be forgotten.

Sharon - Forty-five years, soul sister. You've been a sister, friend, confidante, and constant grace to me. You've loved me when I couldn't love myself. You've given me space to heal and the safety to bloom again. I am endlessly grateful for you. You are loved and appreciated.

My Soul Sisters

Amy Cragg - Salad Sisters forever! You wild, radiant force! You're an inspiration - fierce, funny, and full of heart. Your most recent challenges would have capsized many, but you met them head-on with courage and grace. Thank you for believing in me, giving me many opportunities to grow into confidence. Road trip soon? I love you!

Sandra Phillips (Lee) - why *do* you have an Asian name? Still makes me laugh. When are we renting that Picton apartment again? Karaoke, anyone? You're one of the coolest friends I could ever ask for. Fifty Shades of Orange - unforgettable! I love you.

Desiree Rogers - our bond runs deep and wide. Thank you for being a safe space, always. No judgment - just love. I love you, Paul, and the boys - and I'm so proud of you all.

Shelley Vernon - heartbreak brought us together, laughter and honesty made us family. We both speak fluent nonsense (and wisdom of course), and I wouldn't have it any other way. I love your wit, depth, wisdom and light. Losing our precious Stevie connected us in a sacred way. Namaste.

Debbie Mason - instant connection, endless conversation. Thank you for sharing your heart and your time with me. You're a blessing and inspiration to me and many others.

Cobie Curtis - a wonderful human and a new friendship but you already feel like family (we practically are) I'm so grateful we have crossed paths. You are the best mama-in-law our Shannon could ever have.

To *all* my chosen sisterhood - You know who you are - my circle of laughter, depth, and divine timing. You each are a part of my journey. I am so blessed to have you in my life regardless of distance. Simone, Selena, Jo, Ange, Fiona, Billie, Shannon, Dani, Lisa, Cuzzie Carol-Lyn, Denise, Nicci, Paris, Kara, Leanne, Jo-Jo, Shar, Alannah (sisters from another mother), Kylie, Maggie, Flick, Stacy(sister forever), and Lyn McIndoe (#3 Mama Bear to Stevie), I still have the patchwork quilt you made for him. It goes everywhere I do. Brucie, Aaron & Pete - you would look wonderful in skirts - you belong here.

This book is part of you all as you have enriched my life in ways you may never know.

You are the gentle breeze upon my bloom, the sunlight through my seasons, the living proof that connection heals.

With much *agape,*

Leeanne

www.ingramcontent.com/pod-product-compliance
Lightning Source LLC
Chambersburg PA
CBHW061504050726

47593CB00002B/442